FEB ? 1998

S

D0447043

ENTREPRENEUR MAGAZINE

Human Resources
for Small Businesses

The *Entrepreneur* **Magazine Small Business Series**

DISCARDED
Daly City Public Library
Daly City California

ENTREPRENEUR MAGAZINE

Human Resources
for Small Businesses

William R. Sullivan

John Wiley & Sons, Inc.

New York • Chichester • Brisbane • Toronto
Singapore • Weinheim

S

658.303
SUL

This text is printed on acid-free paper.

Copyright © 1997 by William Sullivan
Published by John Wiley & Sons, Inc.

All rights reserved. Published simultaneously in Canada.

Reproduction or translation of any part of this work beyond that
permitted by Section 107 or 108 of the 1976 United States Copyright Act without the permission of the copyright owner is unlawful. Requests for permission or further information should be addressed to the Permissions Department, John Wiley & Sons, Inc.

This publication is designed to provide accurate and authoritative
information in regard to the subject matter covered. It is sold with
the understanding that the publisher is not engaged in rendering
legal, accounting, or other professional services. If legal advice or
other expert assistance is required, the services of a competent professional person should be sought.

Library of Congress Cataloging-in-Publication Data:

Sullivan, William R.
   Entrepreneur magazine : human resources for small businesses /
William R. Sullivan.
      p.   cm. — (The Entrepreneur magazine small business series)
   Includes index.
   ISBN 0-471-14946-2 (cloth : alk. paper). — ISBN 0-471-14947-0
(pbk. : alk. paper)
   1. Small business—Personnel management.   I. Title.   II. Series.
HF5549.S8978   1996
658.3′03—dc20   96-20540
                                                                       CIP

Printed in the United States of America

10   9   8   7   6   5   4   3   2   1

This book is dedicated to the memory of Anna C. Stetter
and
many thanks to Ashley Vieira.

PREFACE

This book was written to provide small business owners with practical help in administering the human resources function. It is intended for companies large enough to have employees, yet too small to support the expense of a full-time human resources manager.

The people side of operations can be quite a challenge for the entrepreneur whose business is expanding for the first time. Although quite successful on your own, you may find yourself unprepared for the extra demands of hiring and directing employees.

Even if you are an entrepreneur with prior corporate experience, you face this challenge. You must adjust to operating without the support of a human resources or a legal department. You no longer have the structure of well-established personnel policies and procedures to fall back on. Making this transition can be both liberating and, at times, intimidating.

Within certain limits, you can manage your people as you see fit, without having to contend with corporate bureaucracy. On the other hand, responsibility for personnel decisions cannot be shared with your boss, as it was in the old days. The buck stops with you, because you're the boss.

In an era of rapid change and heavy competition, enlightened companies are realizing just how important employees are to the success of their operations. Their value as business assets is perceived from a practical sense, not just paternalistically. It makes good sense to create a healthy working environment.

Treated fairly, most employees will put forth the extra effort and cooperation to do a good job. They'll generate ideas for improvement and own up to their mistakes without fear of intimidation. Operations tend to be smoother, and problems that occur get resolved faster, often without the owner's participation. Frequently, fair and consistent application of effective personnel policies will be reflected in lower turnover, less litigation, and higher productivity.

As an owner, you have a responsibility to foster a good working environment. Over time, your personality and management style will be reflected by your people. Some will absorb your ethics and approach to dealing with problems. This book provides some tools for building your own personnel programs. It makes no attempt to cover all the intricacies of the human resources (HR) field, but it will provide you with the foundation for a good start and will support more advanced programs later on if you expand. Each chapter offers practical information for entrepreneurs, as well as a wrap-up at the end that reviews general guidelines on that chapter's topic.

The HR field is and will continue to be highly regulated. The laws affecting personnel administration are many and are often quite intricate. The author makes no attempt to proffer legal services and throughout the book will refer you to legal counsel when appropriate.

CONTENTS

ENTREPRENEUR MAGAZINE

Human Resources
for Small Businesses

1

THE EMPLOYMENT PROCESS

Hiring people is one business transaction that can't be fully automated. It's different from dealing with vendors, clients, or customers. In a smaller business, it's quite personal. You may spend more waking hours with your employees than your own family. As an entrepreneur, you must depend on other people, initially strangers, to perform services vital to your economic well-being.

Even a background in corporate hiring won't totally prepare you for the experience. It helps, yet there's a difference. The consequences for a bad hire in a big company are not as serious. Big companies can better absorb a mistake. Most likely in a large company you wouldn't lose your job over it. Perhaps the responsibility was spread between you, Human Resources, or a hiring committee. Politically astute, you may have had your boss approve your selection. Your personal stake in the decision was not as deep. How could it be? Back then, you didn't own a business. Now you do. It's no wonder some owners are nervous with the employment function.

It's natural for people to short-circuit any process they're uncomfortable with. Hiring people often tops the list. You want to get it over with as soon as possible. The temptation to make quick decisions is always present. We often succumb to trusting gut instincts and luck. Remember, however, that hiring is like shaving—if you rush it, you'll cut yourself. As with a hasty marriage, you'll repent at leisure.

What is the payoff for a well-planned hiring effort? It makes life easier when you hire good people early on. You'll avoid the myriad of problems associated with mediocre folks, such as low productivity, poor attendance, lousy customer service, theft, and high turnover and injury rates. Poor workers sour your office. They infect the good ones, bringing everyone down, including yourself. And they drain off profits.

Good employees adjust faster to change and work better under less-than-ideal conditions. Self-motivated, they require far less supervision, freeing you up for other matters. With better people, you don't have to be a star owner with tremendous leadership abilities. Show them respect and they'll work around your own shortcomings and cut you some slack when you stumble.

Building good staff is like making homemade soup. The people you hire are the ingredients you mix in. High-quality ingredients guarantee a first-rate meal. The employment process outlined in this chapter is a recipe you can follow. It's not magical. It takes patience and effort to make it work. The sweat equity invested will reap high dividends.

STAFF PLANNING

Before hiring additional staff have you spent some time thinking things through? Do you really need to bring someone else aboard right now? If you're a thoroughly "hands on" entrepreneur and close to the action, the need may be so obvious it doesn't warrant much thought. Nonetheless, answering the following questions may stimulate some creative ideas on your part:

- If a cry for more help is coming from existing employees, do you really have a handle on their current workload? Some simple reports, collected at the end of the day, that summarize the number of calls received, sales calls made, or units completed may confirm or disprove this need, yet it is surprising how many owners have few or no procedures in place to track work volume.

- Would it be more practical to handle increased work with overtime? You may have someone on staff who would jump at the opportunity to make some extra bucks.
- Can some of the added work be redistributed to other employees instead, even if it takes some additional training?
- Can temporary staff fill the need until you get a better handle on it?
- Can a part-time, rather than a full-time person do the work?
- Can work with lesser priority be eliminated or rescheduled, eliminating the need for additional staff at this time?
- Would faster equipment or more modern production tools speed up processing?
- Would it be practical to contract out work to someone on the outside, reducing the need for more staff?
- Have you asked trusted employees for their suggestions?
- Are you ready to admit you may have some so-called turkeys on board who need to shape up or ship out? Perhaps now is the time to address their situation.

As you contemplate these questions, alternatives you never expected may come to mind. A combination approach may evolve. This may be the best time to begin writing job descriptions. The act of writing often helps to crystallize ideas. If you can, write job descriptions using a word processing program, which will allow faster revision. Job descriptions don't take that much time to write, and they serve a variety of purposes, such as the following:

1. They clarify a job into duties and responsibilities. Look at a position from the owner's perspective and ask these questions:
   - What duties need to be done at this level?

- What duties are more important than others? What are *essential* versus *nonessential* duties?
- Is this job exempt or nonexempt? Use the job description for determining exempt, nonexempt status (covered further in Chapter 2).
- Who reports to the worker in this position? Who does the worker report to? Who else besides you does this worker receive direction from?
- Does this job support other jobs as a back-up for illness or vacation? This function may require added skills and job knowledge, indicating a need for additional on-the-job training.

2. What should this job be paid? What is the job worth to your company? What is it worth to your competitors? (These topics are covered in Chapter 2).

3. Once the job is broken down into the duties, responsibilities, salary, and so forth, the job description can be an effective tool for writing ads, recruiting, and interviewing.

4. Job descriptions may help you keep focused on actual skills required, not race, religion, sex, age, or national origin.

Staff and organizational planning should be easy and comfortable; after all *this is your company*. Your people will be your support, your allies, and your subordinates. Remember, organizations are dynamic and need to be evaluated periodically, top-down as well as bottom-up. If you own a franchise, you may already be provided with a basic organization structure with key positions to fill. Listed below are some questions to ask yourself before you begin:

- Do you need a person to greet vendors, customers, and other visitors? What impression do you wish this person to convey? What skills should this person have?
- Do you need an assistant to handle all aspects of your office organization? Should the assistant be full- or part-time? Can the receptionist and assistant be the same person?
- Do you need an inside financial person to handle your accounting and tax needs? Can you support a clerical person

(bookkeeper)? Can your outside accountant fill this need initially?

- Can payroll be done by an outside firm? If you can afford a payroll person, what duties would you wish this person to do in addition to payroll?
- Will you be handling human resources duties yourself? Such duties include maintenance of personnel files, hiring and firing of personnel, policies and procedures development and maintenance, and benefits coordination.
- In your main area of operations, what skills are required? Should there be a supervisor or a senior person who directs others, in addition to regular duties?

There are certainly a lot of questions. Being an entrepreneur isn't all fun and games. Now that you are thinking of (and possibly comatose from) all the possible alternatives, let's look at a simple, functional organization chart in Figure 1-1. Use this very basic table to define positions by combining functions. Use it to get an overview of who should report to whom. Remember, keep it simple!

CREATING JOB DESCRIPTIONS

The general purpose of job descriptions is to define a job with your company by breaking it down into specific functions, prioritizing these functions, and establishing deliverable products such as reports, sales, or assembled products. As the owner, it will be your responsibility to clearly define what each job does, and how it relates to other jobs within your firm so combined efforts are successful. Job descriptions should be created for each new position. For existing positions you should review and update them at least once a year or when any of the following circumstances apply:

- New duties are added to a job; for example, the worker now supervises two people.
- Jobs are combined.
- Jobs are eliminated.

Figure 1-1 Functional Organization Chart

```
                        ┌──────────────┐
                        │     You      │
                        └──────┬───────┘
                               │        ╭──────────╮
                               │        │  Your    │
                               ├────────│ Assistant│
                               │        ╰──────────╯
        ┌──────────────────────┼──────────────────────┐
┌───────────────┐      ┌───────────────┐      ┌───────────────┐
│  Your Finance │      │     Your      │      │     Your      │
│     Area      │      │Administrative │      │  Operations   │
│               │      │     Area      │      │     Area      │
└───────┬───────┘      └───────┬───────┘      └───────┬───────┘
    ┌───┴────┐                 │                      │
┌────────┐ ┌────────┐   ┌────────────┐        ┌────────────┐
│Payroll │ │Business│   │  Clerical  │        │ Sales and  │
│Functions││Accounting│ │  Support   │        │ Marketing  │
└───┬────┘ └───┬────┘   └─────┬──────┘        └─────┬──────┘
┌────────┐ ┌────────┐   ┌────────────┐        ┌────────────┐
│Preparing││        │   │  Supply    │        │ Production │
│Payroll │ │ Taxes  │   │ Ordering   │        │Development │
└───┬────┘ └───┬────┘   └─────┬──────┘        └─────┬──────┘
┌────────┐ ┌────────┐   ┌────────────┐        ┌────────────┐
│Issuing │ │Reports │   │  Human     │        │            │
│Paychecks││to Fed  │   │ Resources  │        │  Assembly  │
│        │ │and State│  │ Functions  │        │            │
│        │ │Agencies│   │            │        │            │
└───┬────┘ └───┬────┘   └─────┬──────┘        └─────┬──────┘
┌────────┐ ┌────────┐   ┌────────────┐        ┌────────────┐
│Answering││        │   │Office      │        │            │
│payroll │ │Vendor  │   │Services,   │        │  Quality   │
│questions││Contact │   │Repairs, and│        │  Control   │
└────────┘ └────────┘   │Office Space│        └─────┬──────┘
                        │Allocation  │
                        └─────┬──────┘        ┌────────────┐
                        ┌────────────┐        │  Testing   │
                        │Mail Services│       └─────┬──────┘
                        └────────────┘        ┌────────────┐
                                              │ Shipping and│
                                              │ Receiving  │
                                              └────────────┘
```

Note: Job descriptions should reflect the required duties for the particular position. Sometimes current employees aren't doing what they should be doing. Keep this in mind when you ask them to list their job duties.

A sample job description format is shown in Figure 1-2.

Figure 1-2   Job Description

Job Description

Title: FLSA Status: _____

General Summary:

Essential Duties and Responsibilities:

Nonessential Duties and Responsibilities:

Job Specifications:

Working Conditions:

The above information has been designed to indicate the general nature and level of work performed by employees within this classification. It is not designed to contain or be interpreted as a comprehensive inventory of all duties, responsibilities, and qualifications required of employees assigned to this job.

Approvals:

Name/Date: _____   Name/Date:_____
Title: _____   Title: _____

Explanation of Job Description Sections

1. *Title.* Choose a label for the job. Titles should be as descriptive of the main function of the job as possible. For example, outside Sales Representative, Receptionist/Switchboard Operator, Mail Clerk, and so forth.

2. *General Summary.* This is an overview of the job that defines the purpose of the job and "who this position reports to."

3. *Essential Duties and Responsibilities.* This job exists to perform a function. What is it, and what expertise is required? The Equal Employment Opportunity Commission lists some factors to consider in evaluating whether a responsibility is essential:
   - The amount of time spent in performing the function
   - The frequency with which the function is performed
   - The consequences of not having a person do this job
   - What holders of the job have done in the past and are doing at present

4. *Nonessential Duties and Responsibilities.* These are additional duties and responsibilities that are not critical to the *main* job. These duties may not occur very often, or could be suspended or delegated to someone else without causing major production or service problems.

5. *Job Specifications.* These are the minimum requirements or qualifications necessary to perform the job, determined by identifying some of the knowledge, skills, and abilities required:
   - *Knowledge* examples could be work experience required, special techniques, special training, certifications, or licenses.
   - *Skills* could be verbal, numerical, keyboarding, reading, and interpersonal skills such as cooperativeness, tact, and so forth.
   - *Ability* could be the ability to concentrate, handle pressure, meet deadlines, and pay attention to detail.

6. *Working Conditions.* Specify the physical environment of the job, for example, dirty, hazardous, hot, cold, lighting conditions, noise levels, and so forth.

RECRUITING SOURCES

Finished with your staff and organizational planning and armed with new job descriptions, let's take a look at places you can go to get the people you need. The number of sources are limited only by your imagination and can range from simply putting a help wanted sign in your shop window to a national search for hard-to-find specialties.

Existing Employees

Moving an existing employee into a new job is a solution that is often overlooked because no one thought to check the skills of current employees or because no employee was an *exact* match for the position. The workers you have now are known quantities, both in terms of their assets and their liabilities. Perhaps they've become too familiar and somehow the thought of bringing in the new holds more excitement. Can you play musical chairs? With a little training could an existing employee fill the position? Why not provide your employees with an opportunity for promotion or lateral transfer to widen their experience and value to your company? Have you asked if anyone is interested?

Employee Referrals

Referrals are an often overlooked source. Seriously consider candidates referred by your better employees; they'll seldom recommend anyone who might embarrass them with the boss. They might recommend their relatives so first clarify your position on nepotism.

Nepotism

Some entrepreneurs have severely restricted the hiring of close relatives, or banned the practice altogether because it got out of hand. Brother and sister combinations, sons reporting to fathers, and spouses working in the same unit may be a benefit in some cases, but not everyone's kid or spouse is going to be an effective performer or fit in with the company. Disciplining or correcting an employee is hard enough without having to deal with bad reactions or hard feelings from that person's mate, parent, or siblings. If you end up terminating an employee's spouse, what impact will that have on the one left behind?

Left unchecked over a long enough period, nepotism has the effect of creating so-called corporate inbreeding, with those in more powerful positions getting their relatives hired over those in the ranks. Qualified minority candidates can easily be left out of the picture.

Referrals from Your Network

Let your customers, vendors, and professional and personal friends know you are looking for someone. Stay alert at Chamber of Commerce meetings, seminars, and social events for prospective employees. Keep your business cards handy and give them to those with potential. You may not have an opening now, but the situation could change so keep an eye out for good people.

Professional and Trade Associations

Many professional and trade associations maintain résumé referral services for their members. At no cost, they will send you résumés of members seeking employment. It's up to you to contact likely candidates and arrange for interviews.

Industry Trade Journals

Trade journals may be an excellent place to run ads. Many have positions wanted sections for people seeking employment. Unlike newspapers, however, they publish less frequently (monthly, bimonthly, or quarterly) so your timing must coincide with their publishing dates.

The Internet

Some firms are posting help wanted notices on the World Wide Web, and local Internet bulletin boards are devoting sections to employment. Individuals seeking employment can post résumés at some net locations. Some of the larger newspapers now run their Sunday classified ads on the Net. If you subscribe to one of the commercial on-line computer services or have direct access to the Internet, consider listing your E-mail address in your ads. Internet-savvy candidates can E-mail their résumés to your computer. Once downloaded, you can review them at leisure. Those that hold your interest can be printed out for further consideration.

Temporary Employment Services

The temporary employment field is highly competitive so don't hesitate to shop around for the lowest fees. The workers a temp service assigns to client companies are the temp services' employees, so the temp company is responsible for paying wages, withholding taxes, unemployment, and workers' compensation insurance. Rates are quoted on an hourly basis with a markup for profit.

There are some drawbacks to using temporary employment services. Their workers may not always be screened properly. The service may send the only person readily available, not necessarily the best one. During their assignments, some temp workers may leave the job with little or no notice for better opportunities elsewhere. This is the downside of dealing with the growing contingent workforce within our society.

One benefit of working with a temp service is the temp-to-hire arrangement. The service assigns someone who is also interested in a permanent position with a good company to fill your job vacancy on a trial basis. If you're pleased with that person's performance, call the temporary service and negotiate a permanent hiring arrangement. The temporary service may charge a transfer fee but that is often waived if you have retained the candidate as a temporary long enough (usually 10 to 13 weeks) for the service to make some profit. These fees are often waived for customers providing repeat business.

The advantage of temp-to-hire is obvious. It gives you time to assess the worker's skills and performance without actually hiring the person. The better services will send you candidates that have been prescreened and with reference checks already completed. They can also administer basic skills and clerical tests when appropriate.

Permanent Employment Agencies

Similar to temp services, permanent employment agencies operate within a highly competitive marketplace. Permanent agencies may quote the traditional employment fee but then, when pressed, offer considerable discounts to get your business. The size of the discount depends on the state of the local economy and/or the specialty you're seeking.

The traditional fee within the industry has been 1 percent per each $1,000 of annual salary, with a cap of 25 or 30 percent. For example, if the salary for the position is $20,000 per year, 1 percent for each $1,000 of the $20,000 adds up to 20 percent; 20 percent of $20,000 is $4,000, the placement fee.

Today, fees within the 10 to 20 percent range are more realistic. Again, it depends on the market and the position sought. Hard-to-find specialties require more research and effort by the agency. Some agencies will also offer volume discounts for multiple placements and fee reductions for prompt payment of placements already made.

In recent years the distinction between permanent agencies and temp firms has become blurred because many permanent agencies have gone into the temp or temp-to-hire business. Often they set up a separate unit specializing in what they call contract services.

Contract Services

Many employment firms have opened separate divisions specializing in providing professional and technical workers on a contract basis. Supplying contract workers for computer programming and engineering projects is quite common, and using contract workers within the human resources field is a growing trend. One national employment firm specializing in placing human resources professionals in both permanent and contract positions is InterSource, Ltd., 72 Sloan St., Atlanta, GA 30075, Tel.: (770) 645-0015.

Newspaper Advertising

Newspaper advertising is expensive. Consider placing ads in smaller, local papers first, as their fees are lower than those of the big city editions. Until you establish good credit, you may have to pay up front. Many will now take your ad copy via fax machine.

Ad Size

Keep your ads small. Large display ads with fancy borders are expensive and often unnecessary. People truly seeking work will respond to both large and small ads, not wanting to miss out on any job opportunity.

Open Ads

If you display your company name and address, be prepared to respond to telephone calls and/or visits from both qualified and unqualified candidates. The resulting disruption is one reason owners resort to a blind ad, which does not list the company name.

Like many other personnel activities the employment process could expose you to potential equal employment opportunity lawsuits. There are people who respond to open ads and later sue if they are not hired or even considered for the position, claiming race, sex, age, or other discrimination. This problem is particularly acute with larger firms perceived as having deep pockets.

An example of an open ad placed in the sales section of the classified ads is provided in Figure 1-3.

Blind Ads

With blind ads you don't list your company name and/or address. For an additional fee, most newspapers will provide one of their own box numbers for ad responses. Another approach is to

Figure 1-3   Open Ad

Recruiter

Seeking professional self-starter for
employment service. Must be well-
organized, previous sales experience
required. Salary plus commission.

Call Joanne at 770-999-9999
or mail résumé to
Staffing, Inc.
90 E. Road
Atlanta, GA 30339

use a U.S. Postal Service box number or rent a box from a local, private firm (e.g., Mailboxes, Etc.). Responses will reach you much faster and most candidates won't find out who you are.

The downside of blind ads is that some qualified people may not respond. They don't wish to send their résumé to a company whose name they don't know. It might be their present employer. How embarrassing! Having spent most of my career in the human resources field, I've seen it happen more than once.

Figure 1-4 shows an example of a blind ad placed in the administrative section of the classified ads, using the newspaper as the return address.

Timing

The Sunday papers draw a heavier response. Avoid holiday weekends if you can; many people travel and may miss your ad.

Fast Fax Response

Increasingly, companies are listing a fax number in their ad. If you do so, ensure your fax machine is loaded with enough paper to handle incoming responses during and after normal working hours, particularly weekends. Once I had an ad response from a candidate who faxed me more than fifteen pages, including every performance review he ever had! See Figure 1-5 for a sample ad with fax number.

Figure 1-4   Blind Ad

Administrative Assistant
To $25,000

Mature professional needed to
assist busy owner with administrative
duties. Strong computer, telephone,
and writing skills a must. Send
résumé with cover letter to:

Ad #4107
Herald Journal
P.O. Box 9136
Syracuse, NY 13027

Running Multiple Ads

When running newspaper ads for different jobs at the same time, you may run into difficulty identifying and sorting incoming résumés. Not all candidates will indicate in their cover letters the specific ad or job to which they are responding. Avoid this dilemma by using a simple identifying code in the ad's return address, for example, initials, abbreviations, or numbers. See Figure 1-6 for a sample multiple ad.

Figure 1-5   Ad with Fax Number

Receptionist
Professional, N. Ga. Location
Handle 12-line phone
Light typing

Fax résumé to: 770-999-9999

Figure 1-6   Multiple Ad

The following positions are
open in our newly formed
insurance agency

Accountant
4+ years' experience
in insurance accounting. Must be computer-
literate. Please forward résumé
and salary history. Indicate code FC.

Financial Assistant
Need good analytical, organizational
skills. PC-literate, Excel 5.0,
agency experience a plus. Send résumé and
salary history. Indicate code FA.

ACME Insurance
200 NW Ave.
Metropolis, NY 10021
Fax: 202-999-9999

Other Sources

State Employment Services

Your state Department of Labor office may be a good source of candidates. Many DOL offices have sophisticated testing services as part of their assessment and placement programs. Put your tax dollars to work.

Local Colleges and Technical Schools

Schools are sources for entry-level people as well as mature workers who go back to school to upgrade skills or jump-start a second career. Consider recruiting students for work on a part-time basis, or for the summer months. You may decide to hire them upon graduation.

Religious Organizations

Many religious organizations run no-cost referral services for out-of-work members.

PREINTERVIEW SCREENING

Résumé Screening

Screening résumés takes time as they come in all styles, lengths, and degrees of readability. You'll accomplish more if you can get away from the workplace and find a quiet place in which to concentrate. Many résumés are professionally written by someone other than the applicant. These are sales pieces designed to secure an interview. Others are homemade and more truly reflective of the candidate. For jobs requiring minimal skills and education you shouldn't expect professional résumés. Applicants may send handwritten cover letters.

Always remember that fraudulent résumés abound. Exaggerated or false information is presented, particularly in the areas of education, levels of responsibility, achievement, and experience. You'll have opportunities during telephone and personal interviews and background checks, to confirm the accuracy of such information.

Résumé Red Flags

Red flags are discrepancies that *might* result in a particular applicant being disqualified for further consideration or warrant further investigation. Some examples are the following:

- *Vague employment history.* It is not uncommon to receive essay-type résumés summarizing past achievements, with little or no reference to prior employers and length of employment. The preferred résumé is one that contains employment history in chronological order, with clear starting and ending dates (month and year).

- *Large gaps in employment.* Large gaps between jobs may indicate underlying problems, but remember that millions of workers have been laid off in recent years through no fault of their own. Finding a job is much more difficult than it used to be. Allowance should be made for applicants who take time off for child rearing or caring for elderly parents. Many workers are going back to school to upgrade their skills so they can get a good job.

- *Frequent job changes.* Many jobs of short duration may indicate problems.

- *Frequent changes in career path.* This could indicate a lack of direction or lack of persistence and goals. Frequent changes are not uncommon, however, for younger applicants who are still seeking a vocation, or workers who have phased out of a dying industry.

- *Sloppy résumés.* Misspelled words, typographical errors, and faded copy indicate a lack of attention to detail and, possibly, the quality of the applicant's work.

- *Résumés with no cover letter attached.* You should expect at least a short cover letter that introduces the applicant, mentions the position applied for, and includes some highlights of the applicant's background that relate to the advertised job.

- *Mirroring.* This refers to résumés that match the ad so closely you think you have the ideal candidate. The applicant may have mirrored your ad, revising the résumé for an exact fit. When screening volumes of incoming résumés, you can easily forget that mirroring is a possibility.

Figure 1-7 shows an example of a questionable résumé that does not provide sufficient background information such as duration at each position, names of companies worked for, and nature of educational background.

Figure 1-8 has an example of a more complete résumé providing information in chronological order by employment dates, and identification of past employers.

Caution: Often, busy interviewers will write notes on résumés or job applications to help with sorting or to highlight applicant characteristics. Be careful what you write. If the résumé is later read by the candidate, you may be embarrassed. Direct or indirect

Figure 1-7   Incomplete Résumé

IMA BOAST
9 Holiday St.
Holiday, SD 55321

Experience
- Held position as Bookkeeper for a start-up company with 110 people in the Southwest. Reported directly to owner. Posted accounts receivables, assisted with payroll as a backup.
- Held position of Accounting Manager for a firm in Oregon. Supervised planning and budgeting. Oversaw establishment of procedures and guidelines.
- Held position of Accountant for a firm in Iowa. Managed all auditing functions.

Education
Post College: attended 1981-1982.
Georgia State University: attended 1981-1982.
Tulane University: attended 1991-1992.

References
Upon request.

Strengths
- Good problem solver.
- Self-starter.
- Team player.
- Detail-oriented.

Figure 1-8 More Complete Résumé

W. Dexter Excell
1365 York Ave.
New York, NY 10021
202-777-0000

ABC, Inc., Atlanta, Georgia: September 1989–Present

Manager, Human Resources
Installation of Human Resources services including Recruitment, PC-based HRIS system, Employee Relations, Benefits Administration, Organizational Development, Wage and Salary Administration, Policies and Procedures, Employee Newsletter. Responsible for Payroll.

Empire Insurance Corp., Syracuse, New York: October 1980–1989

Director, Human Resources
Established and directed full range of HR activities for new start-up division that grew to more than 500 employees: Recruitment, Employee Relations, Compensation (Hay System) Benefits administration, Training and Organizational Development, Payroll coordination, Employee Cafeteria Services. Passed OFCCP audit of Affirmative Action Plan.

Marketing Administrative Services, New York, New York: January 1971–October 1980

Manager
Personnel and Office Administration for Marketing Division Headquarters and **nine** satellite sales offices supporting 450 employees.

Skills and Education

Adelphi University, Garden City, New York: BBA degree, Industrial Management.
Wharton School/International Benefits Foundation: Certified Employee Benefits Specialist (CEBS).
Cornell University, School of Industrial and Labor Relations: Employment Law Certification Program.
Zenger Miller, Inc.: Certified to facilitate Front Line Supervisory Training Programs.
American Compensation Assoc.: Four of seven tests completed towards Cert. Comp. Professional (CCP).
Society for Human Resources Management: Senior Professional Human Resources Certification (SPHR).

PC Skills: WordPerfect 5.1, DOS 6.0, and MacIntosh Operating Systems, Microsoft Word, Spreadsheet, and Database for Windows, Excel 5.0, Ami-Pro, Org. Plus 6.0, Abbra 2000 HRIS system.

---

references to age, sex, race, national origin, religion, and marital status should be avoided. If the candidate files a discrimination charge, such notes can be interpreted as evidence of discriminatory intent on your part. The following are some examples of careless note-taking:

"What age?"   "Too old for us"
"Fat lady in a blue dress"   "Wears cheap clothes"
"Divorced"   "Lives too far away from office"
"Knockout figure"   "Has foreign accent"

The Telephone Screen

Consider qualifying candidates by phone before scheduling personal interviews. Often you can learn enough on the phone to determine who warrants further consideration. Also, the applicant may decide not to pursue the position. You can save valuable time and effort for both yourself and the candidate.

Because many job applicants are currently employed, you may have to do your telephone screening after normal business hours. Once contacted, advise the applicant that you are doing preliminary telephone calls to selected candidates to determine mutual interest. Proceed with your questions, assessing the quality of the person's responses. Close by stating that applicants will be contacted further *only* if they are among the final candidates being considered. Only finalists will be invited to complete an employment application and personal interviews.

The following are sample telephone interview questions.

1. "Briefly go over your last three jobs, telling me one main accomplishment for each job and why you left that job." This question is asked to see if the candidate has the following abilities:
   - Can understand multiple questions
   - Can ask for clarification if the question is not understood
   - Is able to logically go from discussing one job to the next
   - Is able to briefly explain bridges between jobs
   - Can describe what he or she considers an accomplishment
2. "Briefly explain why this position [being applied for] is desirable." This question is asked to see if the candidate can do the following:
   - Articulate why they applied for the job
   - Understand what the advertised job is

The Employment Application

What a pain it is to complete employment applications. Why can't employers just use my résumé? applicants wonder. They then grit their teeth and methodically answer the questions, filling in blanks that are too small to write in. Despite the hassle, the application form does play an important role in the employment process for the following reasons:

- It's the first document an applicant completes on your terms, in your format.
- It captures essential data needed to make more complete candidate evaluations.
- It communicates important legal information designed to protect your company.
- It's a key information source when putting new hires on the payroll.
- It's a form of test to see who can write clearly and follow instructions.

Have faith, eventually this nuisance form will be replaced in our society by interactive computer programs that will capture applicant data on-line. Until this happens, you'll need a good application form for your business.

Although generic forms are available in office supply stores, consider designing one suited to your particular needs. The more data you capture on the form, the fewer routine questions you'll need to ask during the interview. Figure 1-9 shows a basic form you can copy to get started. If you decide to design your own, the information provided in Figure 1-10, "Entrepreneur's Guide to Creating Employment Applications," should prove useful.

Employment applications should be completed by *all* applicants invited for interviews. Insist that it be filled out *completely,* particularly the job history section. Don't permit the applicant to short-cut the process by writing on the application "See résumé." The résumé may not contain all the information you require.

Some applicants may attempt to conceal illiteracy. Some may bring a colleague with them to complete the application on their behalf. This may be understandable but is unfair to the employer. If the applicant has such problems, you should know

Figure 1-9   Employment Application

APPLICATION FOR EMPLOYMENT

We are an Equal Employment Opportunity Employer. Applicants will receive consideration
without regard to race, color, religion, sex, national origin, age, disabilities, disabled or Vietnam
veteran status, marital status, citizen status, or any other protected class.

Name: Last	First	Middle	Social Security Number
Present Address: Street City State Zip			Area Code/Phone Number

Have you ever worked for us before? Yes___ No___ If yes, give dates: From:_____ To: _____
Have you ever been convicted of a felony? (Conviction of a felony is not necessarily a
disqualification for employment)   No ___ Yes____ Explain: _____
Position you are applying for: _____
Date available for employment:_____
Please name any relatives or acquaintances employed by us: _____
Can you provide documentation on your eligibility for residence and employment in the United
States? ____ Yes ____ No.
If under 18, can you furnish a work permit? Yes____ No____

Most Recent: **EMPLOYMENT HISTORY** (Include Military Experience)

Employer	Address City State Zip
Job Title Salary Start Salary End	Supervisor's Name Area Code/Phone Number
Employed from: Part Time ____ Reason for leaving: Mo./Yr. to Mo./Yr. Full Time ____	
Employer	Address City State Zip
Job Title Salary Start Salary End	Supervisor's Name Area Code/Phone Number
Employed from: Part Time ____ Reason for leaving: Mo./Yr. to Mo./Yr. Full Time ____	
Employer	Address City State Zip
Job Title Salary Start Salary End	Supervisor's Name Area Code/Phone Number
Employed from: Part Time ____ Reason for leaving: Mo./Yr. to Mo./Yr. Full Time ____	

Figure 1-9 *Continued*

EDUCATION AND TRAINING		
High School	Course of Study	Graduated: Yes___ No ___
Address		Honors Received
College/Technical/Vocational School	Course of Study	Graduated: Yes___ No ___
Address		Honors Received
College/Technical/Vocational School	Course of Study	Graduated: Yes___ No ___
Address		Honors Received

PROFESSIONAL REFERENCES

Please list **three** business/work references who are **not** related to you and are **not** previous supervisors. If not applicable, list three school or personal references who are not related to you. Indicate in the How Known section what working relationship the individual had or has to you (manager, coworker, customer, user, etc.) and at which company.

Name	Address(City, State, Zip)	Phone Number	How Known	Company
Name	Address(City, State, Zip)	Phone Number	How Known	Company
Name	Address(City, State, Zip)	Phone Number	How Known	Company

PROFESSIONAL ASSOCIATIONS

List professional, trade, business, or civic activities and offices held. (You may exclude memberships that would reveal sex, race, religion, national origin, age, ancestry, handicap, or other protected status.)

CERTIFICATION

I certify the information presented in this Employment Application is correct and hereby give _____ the right to make an investigation based on the information provided. I also understand that misrepresentation of information is grounds for disqualification from further consideration for, or termination from, employment.

I understand I may, if hired, terminate my employment with the company at any time. The company may also terminate my employment and compensation at any time, with or without cause. I understand company personnel or employment recruiters do not have authority to enter into any agreement for my employment for any specified period of time. Nothing contained in this Employment Application, the granting of an interview, or the acceptance of an offer of employment is intended to be construed as a contract of employment.

Signature: _____   Date: _____

Figure 1-10   Creating an Employment Application Form

Entrepreneur's Guide to Creating an Employment Application

A wide variety of application forms are currently in use today. Most have been created to fit the special needs and styles of the particular owner. The data below provides you with more than enough information to design your own application form, capturing the information you'll need to screen applicants and place new hires on the payroll.

Important: Before going to print with your own job application design, be sure you consult with your attorney. Some of the statements in italics have legal implications and are for illustration purposes only. Your attorney will have his or her own approach to such language.

Instructions Section
This section includes routine comments such as "print clearly" and "answer all questions completely." With the passage of the ADA legislation, statements such as the following are also being included.

"If you require accommodation due to a disability in order to complete the application process, please advise us what accommodation you require."

Personal Data
This section includes space for *basic* information such as name, present/permanent mailing address, home and office telephone number, Social Security number. Often included are additional questions which assist in applicant evaluation. Some examples:

- Have you ever been convicted of a felony? If yes, give details, including dates, charges, penalty assessed or disposition. *"Consideration will be given to the nature of the crime, its seriousness, and the position for which you are applying."*
- Have you ever held a security clearance? (For defense contractors).
- Are you acquainted with anyone else in our employ? Who?
- Have you previously worked with the company? When?
- Are you currently employed? With whom?
- May we contact you at work?
- Other names you have been known by?
- Do you have any relatives with our firm? If so, state relationship.
- Have you applied here before?
- Do you have any restrictions on working overtime?

Figure 1-10   *Continued*

- Referral Source: newspaper, agency, friends, relatives, walk-in, other? (Useful when tracking best applicant sources).
- Shift availability?
- Days and hours not available for work?
- Do you have any commitments to or agreements with another employer that might affect your employment with us? (Probing for conflicts of interest or noncompete agreements with prior employers).
- If under 18, can you furnish a working permit?
- Are you a U.S. citizen? If not, do you have the legal right to work in the United States? Type of visa?
- Are you on layoff and subject to recall?
- Will you relocate if the job requires it?
- Will you travel if the job requires it? How much travel?
- Date you can start work?
- Minimum salary required?
- Have you ever been bonded?
- Have you ever been dismissed from employment, forced to resign, or resigned to avoid being dismissed? If yes, please explain.
- Please give your driver's license number, state, and expiration date. Is it currently valid?
- Do you have a commercial driver's license? Number, state, and expiration date.

Type of Work Desired
This information is particularly useful for "walk-in" applicants to confirm what kind of work they are seeking. Example questions:
- Position you are applying for?
- Check boxes for part time, full time, temporary, seasonal.
- Shift? First, second, third, split, or rotating.
- Salary desired?
- Are you able to meet the attendance requirements for this position?

Work History
Allow sufficient room to capture the key data you'll need when checking references. Leave plenty of space for a minimum of four prior employers.
- Name, address, and telephone number.
- Employment dates, (month and year).
- Position held and duties performed.
- Reason for leaving.
- Immediate supervisor (name, title, work telephone number).
- Starting and ending salary.
- Check boxes for part time, full time, or temporary.

(continued)

Figure 1-10   *Continued*

Military Service
Although technically a part of work history, many firms have a separate section in order to obtain additional information such as

- Have you served in the armed forces?
- Which branch?
- Dates (month and year).
- Honorable discharge?
- Final rank?
- Special training received while in the service?
- Are you currently in the military reserve or national guard?

Education
The standard questions are

- Name and address of grade and high school, undergraduate and graduate schools, and other schools (trade, vocational, or professional association schools).
- Course major and minor.
- Number of years completed.
- Dates attended (month and year).
- Did you graduate?
- Degree? Credits received?

Depending on their industry or interest, employers may also include questions on

- Grade point average.
- GED equivalency certificate.
- State certifications, certification number, state, year received, and expiration date.
- Scholastic honors and awards.
- Scholarships, fellowships.
- Memberships in professional and honorary societies.
- Other courses, seminars, specialized training or study.

Note: The years in which an applicant graduated from high school or college are useful when confirming educational references with the schools.
However, it is not recommended that these dates be asked for on the application form itself. It could be construed as an indirect question on the applicant's age, particularly for high school. Obtain these dates after a job offer is made.

Other Skills and Experience
As part of, or separate from, the education section, some owners list questions designed to capture other acquired skills pertinent to their industry or particular job, such as

- Shop skills such as welding, painting, forklift, cranes and hoists, grinders, power tools, electrical, blueprint reading, truck driving.

Figure 1-10 *Continued*

- Typing and shorthand speeds, computer keyboard, PC software, calculator, telephone switchboard, data entry or dictating equipment, filing, fax machine.
- Foreign languages spoken.

Association Memberships
Candidates may be asked to list professional, trade, business, or civic association memberships on the application form. Certain association affiliations have been used by employers to discriminate against applicants, so some firms use statements such as the following:

"Please exclude memberships that would reveal sex, race, religion, national origin, age, color, disability, or any other protected class."

References
Many firms ask for either personal or work-related references on their application forms but usually not both. Business-related references are recommended. The question may be worded as follows:

"Please list three business or work references who have direct knowledge of your skills and abilities. Please indicate the working relationship (manager, coworker, customer, user). List company and title."

Protective Legal Statements
Because of increased litigation, job applications have been heavily weighted with legal jargon necessary to protect the hiring firm. With the exception of the EEO statement, most are located at the end of the form, with acknowledgments and authorizations requiring the applicant's signature.

The EEO Statement
Often located at the top of the application and just below the company logo is a statement affirming that the company is an equal opportunity employer. If sued later for discriminatory hiring practices, EEO agencies may look for such statements; having one may help in the defense. For example,

"We are an Equal Employment Opportunity employer. Applicants will receive consideration without regard to race, color, religion, sex, national origin, disabilities, disabled or Vietnam veteran status, marital status, or citizen status or any other protected class."

Disclaimer of an Employment Contract
The purpose of this statement is to advise applicants that if hired they have no legal employment contract with the employer and can be discharged at any time for any nondiscriminatory reason, with or without cause. This is what is meant by at-will employment. For example,

(continued)

Figure 1-10 *Continued*

"I agree that, if hired, my employment will be at-will and may be terminated with or without notice at any time by me or by the Company. I understand that only a written agreement expressly to the contrary signed by me and by the President of the Company can vary this employment-at-will policy."

Authorization and Release Statement
With this statement the applicant authorizes the company to check references and conviction records and releases all parties involved from liability resulting from obtaining and using the information. For example,

"I authorize my current employer, past employers, educational institutions, and individuals and organizations (including credit bureaus and law enforcement agencies named or referred to in this application to provide the company with references upon request in order to assist the company in deciding whether to employ me. I hereby release my former and current employers, my former educational institutions, and any individual or organization providing such a reference from any liability, damages, causes of action, complaint, or charges concerning the giving and receiving of such references, information, or opinions related to my employment."

Verification Section
The applicant certifies by signature that the information on the application is true and complete:

"I certify that the information provided in this employment application is correct and complete, and I understand that any false information or omissions may disqualify me from employment and, if discovered later on, may justify my dismissal from employment."

Depending on the business needs and individual company policy, employers add other statements to employment applications such as sign-offs for drug testing, physical exams, conflict-of-interest statements, prohibitions of the use of drugs and alcohol at work, statements addressing company policies on proprietary information, inventions, and copyrighted material associated with employment.

---

about them, particularly if adequate reading and writing skills are required to perform the job. *Note:* Reading and writing deficiencies due to disabilities covered under the Americans with Disabilities Act (ADA) are another matter. If the disability is made known to the employer, special assistance or other accommodation may be required to complete the application process. For example, you may provide someone on your staff to complete the application from information provided orally by the applicant.

Except for higher-level positions, insist that all employment applications be completed by the applicant personally at your workplace, preferably under discreet observation. A receptionist or security guard can serve as monitor. Keep your blank application forms secured; don't allow them out of the office.

APPLICANT TESTING

Testing can be an effective tool in candidate selection, training, and placement. The main types of tests are the following:

- *General aptitude tests* are designed to measure general intelligence and/or aptitude for specific functions and are particularly useful in selecting and placing entry-level workers who will require additional training once employed. Such tests focus on measuring logic, verbal, spatial, and arithmetic aptitudes, and ability to learn, understand instructions, adapt, and solve problems.
- *Clerical aptitude tests* measure the ability to deal accurately and quickly with numerical and alphabetical detail.
- *Office skills tests* assess typing, data entry, and ten-key calculator and word processing skills. *Note:* Effective computerized tests are now available to measure these skills.
- *Personality profile tests* are designed to help identify candidates with personality traits compatible with both occupational and organizational demands.
- *Work samples tests* ask candidates to perform tasks that closely match or represent the actual job to be filled. A machine operator may be asked to demonstrate proficiency on the actual equipment, or someone applying for a professional or administrative position may be required to demonstrate specific knowledge by dispositioning simulated work.
- *Honesty and reliability tests* identify those with potential for honesty, emotional stability, reliability, and commitment. These tests became more popular when use of polygraph testing was drastically restricted under the Employee Polygraph Protection Act of 1988. Some tests, however, have run afoul of privacy laws and companies that used them have been sued.

Note: To familiarize yourself with employment tests, consult the yellow pages under Test Publishers—Vocational. There are a number of companies specializing in employment testing, so call for a copy of their catalog and price lists.

Legal Implications

Employment testing, like most other human resource areas, has potential for lawsuits. Be aware of the following:

Civil Rights Legislation

Minority group applicants have successfully sued employers, claiming discriminatory testing practices, particularly where a disproportionate number of minorities were rejected. Many tests have been revised in recent years to eliminate possible racial bias.

Employers bear the burden of proving the test is job related with no viable alternative means of selection. This may prove difficult to substantiate, particularly with general aptitude tests. Because of this, many employers have severely limited or discontinued testing altogether.

Americans with Disabilities Act (ADA)

Special testing arrangements may be required for those applicants who *disclose* to you that they have a disability and require reasonable accommodation to complete both the application and testing process.

Applicants with a visual impairment such as blindness or dyslexia may need a test in Braille, large print, or one given orally by a reader. An individual with a hearing impairment may require a sign interpreter during the interview. Those with learning disabilities may need more time in taking a test. Alternative approaches to the usual testing may be necessary in order to make accommodation, including waiving the test itself.

Preemployment Medical Exams

The impact of the ADA prohibits use of these exams in screening candidates *before* a conditional job offer is made. If considering medical exams, consult with an attorney. *Note:* Drug testing is *not* considered a medical exam for ADA purposes.

Testing for Drugs

Many firms use preemployment drug tests to screen out active users. Remember, drug abusers may be protected under the ADA if they have been or are currently enrolled in a drug or alcohol rehab program and are no longer using these substances.

For small businesses, drug tests may not be worth the expense or risk involved in their administration. You won't hire enough people to warrant their use. Drug testing can be a highly complicated procedure. Also, not all drug use is illegal; many people abuse legal prescription drugs or alcohol. By far, the abuse of alcohol is responsible for more accidents and lost production time than illegal drugs. Legal counsel should be consulted if you do decide to implement a drug testing program.

INTERVIEWING

If you feel interviewing is a chore, you're not alone. Most employers just muddle through. Few managers have ever been trained how to do it properly. Even those who are trained rarely get enough practice.

Interviewing is hard work because it requires extra mental energy to carefully listen to what a candidate says, interpret what is really meant, and observe his or her reactions. Since they're selling themselves, people try to project the most favorable impression possible, keeping negative information to a minimum. You, on the other hand, must discover both positives and negatives in order to reach a hiring decision.

Maintaining Control

During interviews you are closely confined for an hour or more with a complete stranger, probing for critical information on that person's past performance, achievements, education, strengths, weaknesses, level of motivation, likes, and dislikes. To get good results, you have to stay in control at all times. This is not always easy, particularly when interviewing folks with aggressive personalities who try to control the conversation, or those with a tendency to go off on tangents.

Interviewing Takes Effort

It takes effort to watch your tongue, avoiding any comments or questions that could be construed as discriminatory. We all have cultural and personal biases, with a tendency to favor candidates most like ourselves. It takes effort to recognize and overcome these biases so they don't influence our decision. This becomes a greater challenge when interviewing people who belong to groups that frequently suffer employment discrimination in the workplace, such as minority candidates, people from foreign cultures, women, older candidates, persons with disabilities, and so forth.

The stakes are high because a critical segment of the applicant's life—his or her employment—is hanging in the balance. Poor hires may later prove expensive, embarrassing, and painful for both the employer and employee. No wonder business owners and applicants feel discomfort with the process.

Prepare Interview Questions in Advance

Never conduct an interview without a written series of questions to ask all candidates. Sample questions are given later in this chapter. It's very easy to lose control and momentum during an interview. Having a prepared set of questions will help keep you on track. It's fairer to the candidates too, as all will be asked the same core questions.

Do Your Homework

Review the job specifications and résumé once again, keeping a copy on your notepad to refer to during the interview. Go over your list of planned questions, also on your notepad. When the application is completed by the candidate take the time to look it over. Compare the information provided with the résumé, looking for inconsistencies and missing information.

Interview Scheduling

Too often interviews resemble marathons: a long race composed of back-to-back interview sessions. At the end of the day the exhausted interviewer has heard volumes of information from too many candidates. It's difficult to remember who said what. Avoid these problems by following these recommendations:

- If you can, limit yourself to no more than three or four interviews per day so you don't wear down, losing your edge and attention to detail. Allow time between interviews to consolidate your notes and clear your head for the next session.
- Allow time for the applicants to complete the application (about 20 minutes) and undergo any testing before the interview.
- Schedule to avoid having applicants for the same job sitting together in your reception area simultaneously.
- Be willing to interview after hours for those candidates holding day positions with another company.

Interview Objectives

Throughout the interview process, keep in mind that all employment interviews have the following objectives:

- To obtain as much information as possible on the applicant's knowledge, skill level, and ability to do the job.
- To assess if the applicant has the personality traits necessary to succeed in the position.
- To confirm levels of past performance.
- To assess the candidate's levels of maturity and integrity.
- To sell the better candidates on working for the company before making a final offer.

Setting the Stage

Put your telephone on hold or in voice mail mode. Advise others in the office that you are not to be disturbed during an interview.

Preparing the Applicant

Be empathetic and friendly. Offer the applicant a cup of coffee or a soda and ask if he or she needs to use the restroom first. This is a common courtesy that is easy to forget. Use small talk for a few minutes to create a relaxed atmosphere. Avoid interviewing at your desk. Sitting adjacent to the applicant on a couch or at a table is less formal and fosters better communication. The best interviews are more like relaxed conversations.

Mention that you'll be taking notes during the interview and also have a series of standard questions you will be asking all candidates. If you feel you can stay on track, permit the applicant to ask you brief questions during the interview. If the questions get out of hand, politely ask the applicant to hold off until you have finished with your questions.

The Questions

Skilled interviewers rely predominantly on open-ended questions, in other words, those that cannot be answered easily by a simple yes or no. Begin questions with the words *how, what, where,* and *why. Tell me* statements such as the following are also effective for getting candidates to open up:

> *Tell me* about your last job.
> *Tell me* about some areas where you think you can improve professionally.
> *Tell me* about some areas where you think you can improve personally.
> *Tell me* how you went about solving the production problem you mentioned to me earlier.

To avoid monotony, consider combining two or more questions, which should keep the candidate talking for some time while you listen, take good notes, and encourage him or her to continue. Interject when appropriate with follow-up questions, particularly when the answers don't provide the depth you require. For example, "Please *tell me* more about that," and "Please go over your work history starting with your earliest job and moving forward to the present. Please *tell me* a little about each job, *what* you liked the most and the least about it, and *where* you did a great job."

Additional Interview Questions
1. Please summarize your education for me. What courses did you like? Why? What courses did you dislike? Why?
2. How did you get your first job? Why did you choose that company? Why did you leave? Who was your favorite manager or supervisor? Why? What did you learn from your first job? Would you do that job again if you were starting over? Why?
3. How did you get your second job? Summarize your three greatest achievements. What were your worst mistakes? What did you learn from them? Why did you leave that job?
4. Why do you wish to leave your current position?
5. Why does this advertised position appeal to you?
6. In summary, tell me anything else that will help me understand you and your achievements.

Questions, Comments, and Conversations to Avoid during Interviews

Avoid subjects that can be dangerous within the context of antidiscrimination laws. For example, questions or even conversations regarding a person's age, race, color, sex, marital status, religion, and national origin can set the stage for an employment discrimination lawsuit. Questions about where a person is originally from or what foreign languages a person speaks (unless required by the job) could lead to a charge of national origin discrimination.

Under the Americans with Disabilities Act (ADA) it is illegal to ask an applicant if he or she has any disabilities. However, you can ask if the candidate can do the job as explained with or without some sort of reasonable accommodation. For example, "This job requires lifting 40 pounds occasionally and standing on your feet for eight hours. Would this pose any problems for you?"

Avoid questions about prior workers' compensation claims or hospitalizations because they may be construed as attempts to discover disabilities. *Note:* It is not illegal for the applicant to voluntarily disclose disabilities.

With minority and female candidates, common sense and sensitivity on your part is required and will be appreciated by them.

With people of color, avoid trite questions regarding home owner-ship, the neighborhood they live in, or where they were born or raised. With women avoid questions on marital status, or conversa-tions regarding their child care arrangements. Male interviewers should also be wary of comments that could be construed as sexist. For example, calling a woman "honey" or a novice female candi-date "girlie" is inappropriate in this day and age.

Job-Related Questions

Despite the questions to avoid, you still have a wide range to cover during an interview. The key is to keep your questions *job re-lated*. You want to know if the candidates have the knowledge, skills, and experience required to perform the job applied for. Do they have the education or technical training necessary? Do they have the right temperament, the necessary motivation, and the problem solving ability? What about their past job performance?

There is nothing to prevent you from asking tough, detailed questions on prerequisite job knowledge and experience as well as follow-up questions if you get vague or shallow answers. You *can* ask them to tell you about the most difficult boss, subordinate, or coworker they have dealt with, and how they handled that person. You *can* ask how many hours per week they put in on a job, or *why* they were fired, transferred, or promoted to another position. You *can* ask them why they liked or disliked certain people, job func-tions, or work situations. You can even give them hypothetical work problems and ask them how they would go about solving them.

Too Much Personal Information

Some applicants have a tendency to reveal too much personal in-formation, particularly with a good listener! Politely interrupt, steering them back on track with a job-related question. Knowl-edge of private information can be a problem. A candidate not hired may claim later that you rejected him or her because of it.

Keep the Applicant Talking

Ideally, the applicant should be doing most of the talking, perhaps 75 percent, during the interview. Inexperienced interviewers wear themselves out talking too much, permitting applicants to quickly size them up and anticipate the next question. You won't learn much unless the applicant does most of the talking. Once a person opens up you'll be surprised by how much information will be revealed, providing glimpses into underlying attitudes, motivations, likes, dislikes, and so forth.

Listening

During interviews, active listening is critical. Take good notes and let the candidate know you are taking notes. Read between the lines and listen. Probe with questions for more data. Continue with more listening and then more probing. Maintain a professional, nonjudgmental demeanor. Try not to visibly react to negative information. If you show disapproval to something he or she says, the applicant will tense up, get defensive, and perhaps shut down altogether.

Length of the Interview

You'll need at least 45 minutes of interviewing time to get through your questions and establish a good feel for the candidate. With professional-level candidates you may find that one or two hours is necessary.

Closing the Interview

When you are finished with your questions give the candidate an opportunity to ask any final questions. State that you have other candidates to interview and give a reasonable estimate of how long it should take to reach a final decision. Thank the candidate again and escort him or her to the door or elevator. If you think a particular candidate is really terrific and have a few moments, walk that person through some of your operation on the way out. Small talk may again be appropriate, helping both of you wind down.

Interview Notes

Review your interview notes soon afterward. Rewrite them if needed for clarity and neatness. Good notes are useful in helping make a final decision. The act of writing and reviewing them may crystallize your thoughts. Also, they can be vital reference material in documenting why a candidate was rejected, particularly if your decision is challenged legally later on.

FINAL SELECTION

Your decision may require second interviews with final candidates. Now that you've met them personally, follow-up questions can often be done over the telephone. Advise them that you are now asking follow-up questions of final candidates. Proceed with questions specifically targeted to areas requiring more information. Often, these second interviews will confirm which person you want.

If, however, you have doubts or vague misgivings regarding a final candidate, stop! Even if you can't pinpoint what's wrong, your subconscious is telling you something. Listen to it. Don't get impatient and rush a decision because you don't want to spend more time on the process. Terminating a bad hire can cost even more time later on. The best cure for doubts is to see more candidates until you find one who provides a reasonable comfort level. Go back to your résumés, set up more interviews, and keep at it. Also keep in mind that there is no such thing as a perfect candidate. If none of the applicants seems to be appropriate for the job, evaluate the ad. Perhaps you were too general in specifying certain skills and experience.

Reference Checking

Employers have an obligation to perform reasonable checks of a candidate's credentials, ideally, before the candidate is hired. You'll want to know if a person is telling the truth about prior employment, education, salary history, and behavior. Who is this person, really?

Negligent Hiring
From a legal perspective, reference checking has become a two-edged sword. On one side, the employer has the obligation to be diligent in checking the bona fides of the people employed.

There are many court cases in which third parties have sued companies for negligent hiring because the firm employed someone who later caused the third party injury during the course of company business. The person suing the company may claim that had the employer done the proper reference checking, the injury would not have occurred because the employee who caused the damage would not have been hired in the first place.

Defamation

On the other side is the fear of defamation lawsuits filed by former employees. This has made many organizations reluctant to give complete reference information. In order to protect themselves, company policy may be to provide only the former employee's dates of employment and positions held. Some will provide more information if you fax or mail a document (signed by the applicant) releasing the company from any liability.

When asked for reference information on your own former employees, exercise caution, particularly if an individual was terminated under negative circumstances. Any statements you make should be factual, not hearsay. Ensure that you have firsthand knowledge of the facts and are able to substantiate them in court if necessary.

Prior Employment Information

Perhaps the best indicator of a new employee's future behavior is past performance with other employers. What was this person's track record with ABC company? How well did she perform? Was his attendance acceptable? As indicated above, obtaining this information can be quite a challenge. Nevertheless, you should make the effort. It is also important to maintain good documentation of such efforts in the employee's personnel file.

If you obtain reference information over the telephone, note down what was said, by whom, that person's position title, and the date. Sometimes you can get more information by reaching the candidate's prior supervisors directly, bypassing the company's human resources department. Savvy companies, however, have trained their management to refer all reference checks directly to their human resources department, which may want your request in writing with an appropriate release document signed by both you and the candidate. A sample release document is provided in Figure 1-11.

Credit History

Checking a candidate's credit history is recommended only for positions in which employees handle cash or exercise financial discretion, or when personal financial conduct is relevant to the position. Examples include positions involving accounts receivable/payable, payroll, and petty cash, and when hiring a chief financial officer, controller, or accounting manager.

Note: The Equal Employment Opportunity Commission (EEOC) has indicated that minorities and women incur a disproportionate number of poor credit histories. Women are often the victims of a poor credit history because of a spouse. To protect your company and avoid potential unfair impact on protected classes, ensure you have a true business necessity for selecting positions for which credit history will be checked. Also, federal bankruptcy legislation prohibits screening out an applicant or terminating an employee *solely* for incurring bankruptcy. Your actions must be supported by compelling business reasons.

Criminal Records Check

Criminal records checks are often performed for all new hires and are particularly important for jobs requiring close, unsupervised contact with the public. Examples include security guards, hotel/apartment managers with access to resident living spaces, and service people who enter private residences.

Obtaining a *complete*, foolproof criminal records history may be difficult because of the large number of justice systems throughout the nation. City, state, and county records systems are not always consolidated or updated promptly and federal criminal records are restricted.

Note: Some states have laws that prohibit refusing to hire someone just because of a criminal record, so check with your attorney before declining someone who has such a record.

Driving Records

Checks of driving records and driver's licenses are often done for positions requiring the use of a company or private vehicle on company business. Don't forget the clerk who routinely drives to the bank to make company deposits. Check both driving records and driver's license validity.

Education

Verification of education is recommended for all new hires. You may need this confirmation even for the lowest-level person, as it relates to potential for future growth, adaptability to training, and potential for advancement to higher-level responsibilities.

Credit- and Background-Checking Companies

Many companies specialize in background checks as well as financial credit history. Their prices vary depending on the depth of the investigation and cover character checks, employment verification, consumer credit, education, driving records, and criminal records. How much you need will depend on the nature and level of the job.

To protect themselves from lawsuits, these firms will require the applicant to sign a background investigation consent document. (See Figure 1-11.) Companies that specialize in these services can be found in the yellow pages of your telephone directory under Credit Reporting Agencies.

Doing Your Own Checking

To save money, you may choose to do some of your own checking. The *Guide to Background Investigations* has a wealth of information on how to go about it, plus reference sources. For more information, write to: the National Employment Screening Services, 8801 S. Yale, Tulsa, OK 74137.

Handling Negative Reference Information

How you handle negative feedback obtained from reference checks will depend on the nature and seriousness of the information, as well as your own sense of propriety. Outright lying on an application or résumé is one thing, exaggerating a bit might be something else.

With a criminal conviction, the approach you take could depend on the nature of the offense and its timing. How long ago was it? Has the person a clean record since then? Does it relate to the job being performed?

How would you handle negative feedback on prior performance? What if the person has already started working and is doing a good job? Do you let that person go or give him or her a chance?

Figure 1-11   Background Investigation Consent Form

BACKGROUND INVESTIGATION CONSENT

I, _____ , hereby authorize _____
and/or its agents to make an independent investigation of my background,
references, character, past employment, education, criminal or police
records, including those maintained by both public and private organizations and all public records for the purpose of confirming the information
contained on my application and/or obtaining other information that may
be material to my qualifications for employment.

I release _____ and/or its agents and any person
or entity that provides information pursuant to this authorization from any
and all liabilities, claims, or lawsuits in regards to the information obtained
from any and all of the above referenced sources used.

The following is my true and complete legal name and all information is
true and correct to the best of my knowledge.

_____
Full Name (please print)

_____
Maiden Name or Other Names Used

_____
Present Address   How Long?

_____
City/State   Zip

_____
Former Address   How Long?

_____
City/State   Zip

_____
Driver's License Number   State of Issue

_____
Date of Birth   Social Security Number

_____
Signature   Date

Perhaps you'll extend the initial employment period, buying more time to make an assessment. Making these decisions is not always easy. Jobs are important, but so is running a good business.

Making the Job Offer

Job offers are frequently made over the phone. It's one of the happier moments in business. Advise the chosen candidate that you'll mail an offer letter confirming compensation, start date, duties and responsibilities, reporting lines, and other pertinent information. In the interest of time, your new hire may wish to drop by to sign the letter in person. Enclose an original and one copy, requesting that the candidate sign the copy for your main personnel file and keep the original.

A good offer letter can prevent many misunderstandings later on regarding compensation, bonuses, benefits, and so forth. See Figure 1-12 for a sample offer letter. It may prompt further discussion regarding terms and conditions of employment, with revisions required. Since offer letters can commit you legally, be sure your attorney approves of the letter format ahead of time.

Rejection Letters

Timing is essential for rejection letters. For those applicants *definitely* not being considered, don't delay; send rejection letters quickly. The letter closes the loop and avoids unnecessary follow-up calls by applicants. You may delay sending rejection letters to your second choice candidate until the finalist has actually started work. You may need your second choice if your primary choice declines the job at the last minute. Waiting may not be fair, however, if an extended start date is involved.

If you ran a blind ad, it is logical to send rejection letters to only those respondents actually contacted and interviewed. A letter should go to all candidates who responded to an open ad identifying your company (see Figures 1-13 and 1-14). The reply will be appreciated, and it helps your public image.

Figure 1-12   Sample Job Offer Letter

On Company Letterhead

Dear _____ :

This letter will confirm our employment offer for the position of Stock Clerk reporting to Ms. Jane Smith, Office Administrator. The starting date will be Monday, July 8, 199__. The salary for this position is $615.38 bi-weekly and the regular work hours will be from 8:00 A.M. to 5:00 P.M., Monday through Friday, with overtime as required.

Your primary duties within this position will be the timely and accurate stocking of inventory and other duties as assigned.

Included in this offer is participation in our group health, life, and dental insurance programs as outlined in the attached benefits brochure. The company pays for 80 percent of the group premium, with the employee paying the remaining 20 percent via bi-weekly payroll deduction. Coverage for eligible dependents is available at full cost to the employee at the group rate. Insurance benefits commence the first of the month following your start date.

This offer is contingent upon the successful completion of the 90-day initial training period and the receipt of positive responses to both background and reference checks. As an "at will" employer, however, the company reserves the right to terminate employment with or without cause at any time.

If you accept this offer, please keep the original for your records, sign the copy where indicated and return to my office. I wish to welcome you to the _____ company and wish you success in your new position. Please don't hesitate to call me with any concerns and questions you may have.

Sincerely,

A. J. Jones, Owner

_____

(Accepted)

Figure 1-13   Sample Rejection Letter (Interviewed Applicant)

On Company Letterhead

Dear _____:

The opportunity to interview you for the position of Stock Clerk was most appreciated. Recently, however, the selection process was completed and another candidate whose credentials more closely match the position's requirements was selected.

Your application will be maintained on file for a period of six months, and you will be contacted if an appropriate opening develops during that time.

Thank you for your interest in the _____ company. We wish you well in your future career pursuits.

Sincerely,

A. J. Jones, Owner

Figure 1-14   Sample Rejection Letter (Applicant Not Interviewed)

On Company Letterhead

Dear _____:

Thank you for your response to our recruitment advertisement for the Stock Clerk position with our company.

We have reviewed your résumé carefully. However, we have recently filled this position with a candidate whose background more closely meets our job requirements.

Your résumé will be maintained on file for a period of six months, and we will contact you if an appropriate opening develops during that time.

We sincerely appreciate your interest in the _____ company and wish you well in your future career pursuits.

Sincerely,

A. J. Jones, Owner

The Trial Employment Period

Commonly set at 90 days, the trial period alerts the employee that during this early phase the company may decide to terminate the new person without going through traditional progressive discipline procedures (i.e., verbal and written warnings). Eligibility for insurance and other benefits may depend on successfully completing this period.

This trial period was often referred to as the probationary period for new employees, however, some courts had interpreted the term to mean that once the period is completed, permanent employment status went into effect with discharge only for good cause. As a result, employers have been changing to terminology such as trial period, training period, or initial employment period.

Guidelines for Entrepreneurs and Small Business Owners

The Employment Process

Let's be realistic, the entrepreneur running a fast-paced business won't have the time to apply all the techniques covered in this book. You'll do the best you can with what little time you do have, so try to focus on the key points listed as follows.

- Consider hiring a college student on an hourly part-time basis to write your job descriptions. Contact the college placement office and seek students majoring in English, journalism, or business.
- Whenever appropriate, bypass the recruiting process by using temp-to-perm arrangements with a local employment service. Let them test, screen, and check references on prospective candidates. Make a final offer only after the temporary employee has thoroughly proved him- or herself on the job. If the temp is not working out, let the service make the necessary replacements.

When doing your own recruiting, do the following:

- Ask your better employees for referrals first.
- If you place a newspaper ad, use a blind ad to prevent being bombarded by telephone calls.
- Screen candidates over the telephone before inviting anyone in for a personal interview.
- Unless you have plenty of experience interviewing people, never do an employment interview without preparing a list of questions ahead of time.
- Have a trial employment period of at least three months for all new people. The time passes quickly, so make the effort to evaluate their performance during that time.

2

COMPENSATION

How much should you pay your employees? Other than being determined by the minimum wage, union-negotiated rates, or prevailing wages specified by government contracts, pay levels for smaller businesses are usually market driven by local industry competition. Base wages are important in attracting and retaining good employees. Paying too far *below* the market is an invitation to trouble. Unless offset by other valued working benefits, such practices detract from rather than support your business. Any money saved skimping on base pay is quickly offset by the added recruiting costs associated with high turnover. If good people are employed, they don't stay long; they move on to better-paying positions with your competitors.

When determining base wages, don't lose sight of important nonwage benefits that help attract and retain employees. From a total compensation perspective, these nonwage benefits should be factored in during your evaluation:

- Will you provide benefits such as health, life, disability, and dental insurance? Employer-sponsored savings plans? If there is a standard for your industry, what is it?

- Take into consideration the growth and stability of your industry.
- The job title and status of the position may be important to many employees, as well as the nature of the work itself.
- The company's location is another factor. Is it in a better neighborhood or an area where safety is a concern? How far will workers have to commute? Is there lots of traffic?

DETERMINING PREVAILING WAGES

Many sources are available for determining prevailing wages at the local, state, and national level. Here are a few:

- *The Bureau of Labor Statistics (BLS).* Annual wage surveys are conducted for jobs in different cities, including professional, administrative, technical, clerical, and maintenance positions. BLS also publishes wage surveys for specific industries such as iron and steel, air carriers, computer/data processing services, health care, and the hospitality industry.
- *Department of Labor (DOL) Offices* (both local and state). Look in the blue pages of the telephone directory. The DOLs have units that specialize in gathering wage information for a variety of benchmark jobs including many within the blue collar category. Speak with one of their wage analysts; most are extremely helpful and provide valuable survey statistics either free or at nominal cost. Put your tax dollars to work!
- *The Local Public Library.* Ask for publications such as the *Occupational Outlook Handbook* published by the U.S. Department of Labor. It contains wage data for many occupations and also includes a directory of state and local government sources of wage information. By the way, you may find that befriending the reference person at your local library is one of the best investments you can make. Most are a wealth of information and will be glad to help entrepreneurs with all sorts of business-related information.
- *Trade Association Groups.* Most professional and trade association groups are listed within the Directory of Association

reference books maintained by your public library. Many of these groups develop wage survey data for their specialties.

- *Local Chambers of Commerce.* The larger ones may publish local wage data for their area.

- *The American Management Association (AMA).* 135 W. 50th St., New York, NY 10020-1201. Tel: 212-586-8100. Fax: 212-903-8168. The AMA has issued a wide range of compensation data covering management, data processing, and professional and secretarial positions.

- *The Administrative Management Society (AMS).* 1101 14th St. NW, Ste. 1100, Washington, DC 20005. Tel: 202-371-8299. The AMS publishes surveys on management, data processing, and office and clerical positions.

- *The American Compensation Association (ACA).* 14040 N. Northsight Blvd., Scottsdale, AZ 85260-3601. Tel: 602-951-9191. Fax: 602-483-8352. The ACA keeps tabs on a wide variety of surveys produced each year.

- *Local ACA Chapters.* The membership of local ACA chapters is made up primarily of compensation specialists working for companies within the community. Contact the local chapter president for local survey sources; some may produce their own surveys for "benchmark" positions. If you need a compensation consultant, they may have a list of available people.

- *National Employment Agencies.* Some publish survey booklets on popular benchmark positions, providing them free to promote their business. For example, Robert Half, Inc. publishes a free booklet on wages for the more common accounting/bookkeeping positions.

- *Consulting Firms.* Although expensive for a smaller business, surveys covering a wide range of positions are sold by firms such as Coopers & Lybrand, Ernst & Young, The Hay Group, Hewitt Associates, William M. Mercer, Towers Perrin, The Wyatt Company, Buck Consultants, and Abbott, Langer & Associates. Costs range from $800 to $1,000. Ouch!

- *Business & Legal Reports (BLR).* 39 Academy Street, Madison, CT 06443. Tel: 203-245-7448. Survey data is available for various positions, reported by state.

- *Personnel Systems Associates.* 2282 Aspen St., Tustin, CA 92680. Tel: 714-573-9430. PSA publishes *Survey Sources* containing the names of hundreds of various compensation surveys produced nationwide, providing title, industry, name, address, and phone number of the organization publishing the survey. The cost is approximately $200.
- *Franchisers.* If you bought a franchise, your franchiser may provide wage data as part of the franchise package.
- *Business Customers/Vendors.* Don't overlook business contacts such as client customers or vendors from the larger companies, particularly those with human resources departments. They may be happy to share some of their own survey statistics.

Wage Surveys

Wage surveys come in a wide variety of formats. Surveyors take different approaches to collecting, analyzing, and publishing their statistics. It's best to review more than one survey from different sources so you can cross-check the results, discounting those that seem way out of sync with the others.

Local area surveys are best for lower-level positions; regional data are used for professional, technical, and middle-management jobs. National survey statistics are often used for top executive and professional positions. The titles included in wage surveys are for benchmark jobs common to industry. Being so common, they lend themselves to comparisons among organizations. The following are examples of some benchmark jobs:

Accountants and Auditors	General Office Clerks
Restaurant and Food-Service Managers	Machinists
Licensed Practical Nurses	Billing Clerks
Bookkeepers	Millwrights

Wage Survey Statistics

Survey statistics can be combined in different ways depending on the type of survey or industry. An excerpt from a typical local area survey is shown in Figure 2-1. It illustrates the wages being paid for Warehouse Supervisor in the Atlanta area.

Figure 2-1   Sample Wage Survey

Warehouse Supervisor

Number of Firms	Incumbents	25th Percentile	Average	Weighted Average	75th Percentile	Low	High
33	51	$25,000	$31,479	$31,859	$37,000	$19,400	$55,000

Warehouse Supervisor—Responsible for the direction and control of raw materials and/or finished goods and for training and developing subordinates. Maintains inventory and inventory records.

- **Number of Firms:** 33 companies participated in the survey by supplying the wages paid for their Warehouse Supervisor position(s).
- **Incumbents:** Within the 33 firms were a total of 51 persons with Warehouse Supervisor jobs.
- **25th Percentile:** 25% of the supervisors in the survey make less than $25,000. This could be useful information for a small business, particularly if money is a problem and you cannot afford to pay higher wages.
- **Average:** The average wage paid for surveyed Warehouse Supervisors. It is a simple arithmetic average the surveyors calculated by adding a set of wages and dividing the sum by the number of wages in the set. It is also know as a *mean*.
- **Weighted Average:** The surveyors weight each individual average by the number of positions that made up that average. Also known as the *weighted mean*. Often, for survey purposes, the weighted average is a more accurate representation of average pay. If you wish to pay your Warehouse Supervisor the local average wage, this is a good figure to go by.
- **75th Percentile:** 75% of the employees in the job make less than $37,000. If you plan to pay above-average wages, but not the highest, this is a good figure to know and understand.
- **Low:** The lowest wage reported in the survey, the very bottom of the pile. The person in the job may be in training or does not have much experience, or this may be a really low-paying company. Perhaps the job responsibilities are lighter than those of most of the other positions. With survey data you really won't know because information like that on individual positions is either not disclosed or is kept confidential.
- **High:** The highest wage reported in the survey, the one leading the pack. Again, survey data does not tell you everything. The incumbent (person in the position) may have moved to the top of the range or may work for a large operation and may have many additional responsibilities and more staff to supervise. You really can't know for sure.

Note: Many surveys also include the *median* wage. The median is the middle number when the pay rates are ranked from high to low. The median wage is usually close to the average or weighted average figures.

It is common for surveys to include the following information:

- *Number of Companies Participating*—those companies that responded by completing the survey questionnaire by supplying their own wages for matched benchmark jobs. Their data are merged with data from other participating firms for the final report. For privacy and competitive reasons, individual company statistics are kept confidential by the organization doing the survey. Some surveys, however, provide a listing of all participating companies by name. Knowing what companies are included may help confirm whether the survey is appropriate for your business. Survey data are often broken down further by size of company, national, regional, and city locations, as well as sales volume.

- *Number of Incumbents*—the number of employees within each position surveyed. Generally speaking, the higher the number, the more valid the data. You may wish to exclude from your evaluation those positions containing too few incumbents. The data may not represent accurate prevailing wages for the position.

- *Average Wages*—a simple average obtained by adding a set of salaries and dividing the sum by the number of salaries in the set. It is also known as the mean or arithmetic average.

- *The Weighted Average Wage*—an average wage composed of each individual position reported in the survey. The difference between a simple average and weighted average is illustrated in Figure 2-2.

- *Percentiles*—distributions used to separate information into definable segments, such as the 25th, 75th, or 90th percentile.

- *The Median (or Middle) Wage*—the number, when the survey data is arrayed from high to low, that splits it in half.

- *The Middle 50 Percent (Interquartile Range)*—obtained by excluding the highest 25 percent and lowest 25 percent of wages reported. The exclusion of the highest and lowest quartiles removes wages of trainees and overpaid people, thus eliminating the extremes.

- *Bonus Data*—often provided for those survey positions eligible for bonuses. Average dollar amounts are given, as well as the number or percent of companies involved.

Figure 2-2   The Weighted Average Wage

Position: Accounts Payable Clerk				
Participating Firms	Average Wage		Number of Workers in Position	Weighted Amount
ABC Company	$16,000	×	1	$16,000
Acme Const	$20,000	×	3	$60,000
Joannes Ins.	$24,000	×	2	$48,000
	$60,000		6	$124,000

Average: $60,000 ÷ 3 = $20,000   Weighted Average: $124,000 ÷ 6 = $20,667

Analyzing appropriate survey statistics should put you in a much better position to develop your own wage scales. You now have some idea what other companies are paying their people for similar positions. Your final decision, however, may also be influenced by the following five factors.

Your ability to pay. Hopefully you'll have the ability to pay a wage somewhere around the weighted average to stay competitive. If not, necessity will dictate a lower dollar amount.

The value of the position. How important is the position to your operation? If it's a critical job you may want to pay a higher starting wage to attract the best people, somewhere above the average, perhaps.

The current labor market. Rapidly changing conditions may influence your decision. Many months may have passed since the survey statistics were first collected and published. In the interim an economic slump may have driven down wages, or perhaps business expansions absorbed excess workers, driving up the rates required to attract and retain workers.

Turnover and morale. If your turnover is high, is it due to the wages being paid? Granted, turnover in industries with historically low-paying jobs will be high. If your business is not in that category, yet you still have high turnover, it may be due to your base wages.

Your own personal philosophy. As an entrepreneur, what reputation do you want in the community? Low payer, middle-of-the-road, or on the high side? In the early years you may start with low wages, moving up the scale, depending on how successful your business becomes.

WAGE RANGES

As your company grows in size and complexity, you may decide to develop formal wage ranges for each of your positions. Formal wage ranges have a number of useful purposes:

- They aid in controlling wage costs. With set ranges, you'll know in advance the most money you'll pay for a particular job.
- When recruiting new people, a set range means you'll know the minimum starting wage for the position.
- They are a good employee relations tool. With defined ranges, employees are less likely to feel that their wages are set out of thin air, at the whim of the entrepreneur. Their wages are determined by a formal process based on prevailing wages within your locale.
- They provide a legal defense. Wages based on formal ranges developed from valid area surveys are less likely to be challenged by discrimination complaints.

Wage ranges are constructed from statistics extracted from wage surveys and are made up of three fundamental components: (1) the minimum, (2) the midpoint, and (3) the maximum.

1. *The range minimum.* The range minimum is the lowest rate you will pay for a particular position. Traditionally, new hires will start at the minimum because they have the least experience. If qualified, they should be able to perform at least 75 percent of the job under normal supervision. Ideally, the range minimum should be high enough to attract *most* qualified candidates to the position. Occasionally, exceptions (wage offers above the minimum) will be made to attract candidates with exceptional qualifications.

2. *The range midpoint.* The range midpoint is the rate halfway between the minimum and maximum of the wage range. Ideally, workers at the midpoint can perform all required job functions with little supervision.

3. *The range maximum.* The maximum is the highest rate paid for a particular position. Technically, employees who reach

their maximums are no longer eligible for raises. They've reached the high end of the wage scale and have "maxed out." They must be promoted or transferred to another position with a higher range to be eligible for a raise, or wait for their existing range to be reevaluated to adjust for inflation or additional responsibilities.

Wage ranges can be derived from the *average, weighted average,* or *median* statistics extracted from appropriate wage surveys. The example in Figure 2-1 provided a weighted average for Warehouse Supervisor of $31,859. The range spread is the percent between the maximum and minimum of the wage range. Traditional range spreads can be anywhere between 35 and 50 percent. We'll use 40 percent in the calculations illustrated in Figure 2-3.

The final range for Warehouse Supervisor is as follows:

- *Minimum:* $25,487
- *Midpoint:* $31,859
- *Maximum:* $38,231

Existing Wage Ranges

You may have access to existing ranges being used by another company within your industry. In order to determine a range spread

Figure 2-3 Calculating Range Spreads

To calculate a 40% range spread, split the 40% in half: 20%

For the range maximum, add 20% to the weighted average of $31,859:
$31,859 × 0.20 = $6,372 $6,372 + $31,859 = $38,231 (range maximum)

For the range minimum, subtract 20% from the weighted average:
$31,859 × 0.20 = $6,372 $6,372 − $31,859 = $25,487 (range minimum)

A faster method:
$31,859 × 1.20 = $38,231 (range maximum)
$31,859 × 0.80 = $25,487 (range minimum)

Figure 2-4 Determining the Range Spread from the Existing Range

Spread = $\dfrac{\text{Maximum - Minimum}}{\text{Midpoint}}$

For example:

$\$38,231 - \$25,487 = \dfrac{\$12,744}{\$31,859} = 0.40$

percentage from an existing wage range you can apply the formula in Figure 2-4.

Updating the Wage Range

Time and market conditions will make it necessary to update your wage ranges periodically. This can be done by estimating a percentage increase for the range, say 4 percent to adjust for inflation. First increase the midpoint by the desired percentage. Once you have a new midpoint, recalculate the new range as indicated in Figure 2-5.

Employees Above or Below the New Wage Range

When installing ranges for the first time it is not uncommon to find that some employees have wages that fall below the minimum for

Figure 2-5 Updating Salary Ranges

Mimimum	Midpoint	Maximum
$25,487	$31,859	$38,231

Range Midpoint: $31,859 × 0.04 = $1,274
$31,859 + $1,274 = $33,133 − new midpoint

$33,133 × 1.20 = $39,760 new maximum
$33,133 × 0.80 = $26,506 new minimum

Adjusted Range:

Mimimum	Midpoint	Maximum
$26,506	$33,133	$39,760

the new range. Less frequently, some salaries will fall above the range maximum. In compensation terms, these situations are called green circle rates and red circle rates.

Green circle rates—indicate those employees whose wage rate falls below the range. Adjusting their wage to the range minimum is in order. If the gap is substantial and money is tight, you may choose to move them up in stages. Provide a partial raise now, and make another installment in six months if competent performance is sustained. Advise the employee and follow up periodically. It is not recommended that you wait too long in moving employees to range minimums.

Red circle rates—indicate those employees whose wage rate is above the range maximum. This is a common problem with traditional wage range systems as employees eventually max out. With the stars, promotion into a higher position and range may be possible, or their present position may be expanded with added responsibilities. Often, the employee may have to wait until ranges are eventually upgraded to reflect inflation and market conditions calling for higher ranges. Care is required in making these decisions as employee morale is at stake. You must balance the need to conform to a fairly established range structure while being flexible under the right set of circumstances. What is right will depend on the circumstances and the organization. If you invade range maximums, you undermine the overall purpose of the program which is primarily salary cost control.

WAGE ADMINISTRATION

From the employee's perspective, effective wage administration means getting paychecks on time, including any scheduled raises when due. To the employer it involves a whole host of time-sensitive operations including:

- Processing tax withholding changes
- Depositing payroll withholding taxes
- Processing overtime wages
- Adding new hires to the payroll
- Deducting any employee-paid portions of group benefits
- Deducting monies to cover wage garnishments

- Processing terminations
- Making raise and promotion adjustments

In addition, bonus pay installments may have to be calculated and paid when due. Payroll processing may have to be coordinated with any performance reviews scheduled. Wage rates must be reviewed and periodically adjusted; wage ranges, if you have them, may need to be updated. Wage rates must be set for new jobs. Wages for existing jobs may require reevaluation if many changes in job content have taken place.

All of these activities are pure overhead, like heat, light, and electricity. With the exception of bonus payments linked to good performance, they have only an indirect relationship to sales, production, or customer service. On the other hand, if not done in a timely manner, problems with morale could result, which could eventually impact your bottom line.

Exempt or Nonexempt Status

This status must be determined to comply with minimum wage and overtime regulations under the Fair Labor Standards Act of 1938 (FLSA). FLSA law covers areas such as minimum wage, child-labor restrictions, and those categories of positions where *overtime* pay is or is not required. This act covers most employers.

Nonexempt Employees

Employees within the nonexempt category must be paid overtime for all work performed above 40 hours during the workweek. Nonexempt employees fall into the following general categories:

- Semiskilled workers
- Unskilled workers
- Clericals
- Technicians

The overtime rate. Any hours over 40 in a workweek are considered overtime hours. The overtime rate is 1.5 times the regular hourly rate.

The workweek. Under FLSA the workweek encompasses a *consecutive* seven-day period adding up to 168 hours ($7 \times 24 = 168$).

Any hours worked over 40 during this period require overtime pay.

Hours worked. Under FLSA, only actual hours worked need be counted in order to determine overtime eligibility. Employers are not required to include sick time, holiday pay, vacation days taken, or meal periods of 30 minutes or more.

Under FLSA, hours worked include both the time you require employees to come to work (normal business hours) and the time you permit them to be on duty or at work. There is a difference between *requiring* and *permitting* someone to work. Some employees may voluntarily come in early and leave late. They don't want overtime pay; they're just conscientious. A grateful employer permits them to do so, unknowingly incurring an overtime obligation for hours worked beyond the 40-hour limit. If later reported to the Labor Department, the employer can incur back pay obligations and fines, and even criminal penalties for serious and deliberate violations.

Exempt Employees

You *are not* required to pay overtime for employees within the exempt categories. The difference between exempt and nonexempt workers is determined primarily by their job duties and responsibilities. The exempt categories are as follows:

1. Executives
2. Administrative employees
3. Professionals
4. Outside sales workers

The U.S. Department of Labor (DOL) also specifies pay level requirements for the executive, professional, and administrative categories. However, since they have not been updated to account for inflation they have lost much of their value as a criteria, and so are omitted here.

1. *Executives.* According to DOL guidelines, to qualify as an executive the employee's primary duties must include:
   - Managing the company or a unit within the company and directing two or more workers.
   - The authority to hire, fire, or recommend hiring or firing workers.

- Regularly making important decisions affecting operations.
- Devoting *no more* than 20 percent of job time to nonmanagerial duties (40 percent for executive positions in retailing).

In addition to the functions involved with hiring and firing, the DOL has provided the following examples of duties that are managerial and supervisory in nature:

- Setting and adjusting pay rates and work hours.
- Directing, planning, and distributing the work.
- Determining work techniques.
- Keeping production records of subordinates.
- Evaluating employee efficiency.
- Handling employee complaints.
- Controlling workflow.

2. *Administrative employees.* Employees in this category have the following duties and responsibilities:

- Responsibility for office or nonmanual work directly related to the running of the business. An example is the executive assistant working closely with the owner.
- Regularly show independent judgment in making important decisions.
- Regularly assist the owner, president, or other administrative employees.
- Perform work requiring training, experience, and knowledge under only general supervision.
- Do not spend more than 20 percent of work time on nonexempt work.

   Some examples of administrative employees include:

- Executive and administrative assistants.
- Assistant buyers in retailing.
- Staff people who are advisory specialists for management.

3. *Professional employees.* Professionals include the so-called learned, the artistic, and the teaching professions. Following are some of their duties:

- Performing work requiring advanced knowledge in a field of science or learning, and requiring prolonged study.

- Performing work that depends primarily on the employee's invention, imagination, or talent.
- Performing work that is predominantly intellectual and varied, as opposed to work that is routine or mechanical.
- Not spending more than 20 percent of job time on duties not in the professional category.

  Some examples of fields employing professionals are the following:

- Law and medicine.
- Accountancy and actuarial science.
- Engineering and architecture.
- Physical, biological, and chemical sciences.
- Certified medical technology and pharmacy.

4. *Outside sales personnel.* Outside salespeople are exempt if they regularly work *away* from the employer's place of business. Their duties include:

- Selling tangible or intangible items such as goods, insurance, stocks, bonds, or real estate; or obtaining orders or contracts for services or use of facilities, such as radio time, advertising, typewriter repairs
- Not spending more than 20 percent of their job time in activities other than those listed above

The following includes common job titles found within the exempt and nonexempt job categories:

Exempt	Nonexempt
Chief Financial Officer	Receptionist
Controller	Mail Clerk
Corporate Attorney	Plumber
Underwriter	File Clerk
Employment Counselor	Maintenance Person
Engineer	Electrician
Executive Assistant	Computer Repairer
Administrative Assistant	Assembly Line Worker

For additional information regarding exempt/nonexempt classifications, contact your local U.S. Department of Labor office. Ask for:

- WH Publication 1363—Executive, Administrative, Professional, and Outside Sales Exemptions under the Fair Labor Standards Act
- WH Publication 1282—Handy Reference Guide to the Fair Labor Standards Act

Compliance Problems

For generations, employers have had problems with the exempt/ nonexempt system. Gray areas exist and positions can be misclassified. Many businesses purposefully misclassify nonexempt positions as exempt to avoid paying overtime. Department of Labor auditors focus on the *actual duties* for a particular position. They are not easily fooled by fancy position titles, but look closely at the actual work being performed. Misclassifications can result in back pay liabilities, including fines.

Employees react differently to their FLSA status. Nonexempt workers putting in heavy overtime may pass on a promotion to an exempt-level position, because such advancement means loss of overtime pay. However, they may actually lose money in doing so. Other employees will welcome getting a supervisory job, enjoying the higher status it may bring, even though they are no longer eligible for overtime pay.

Written during the Depression over 50 years ago, the Fair Labor Standards Act needs an overhaul. Back in 1938 the differences between workers and the supervisory staff were more clearly defined. Manufacturing predominated, with higher proportions of blue-collar workers cranking out tangible products. In today's service-oriented economy, with flattened hierarchies, the distinctions are less pronounced. The demands for hands-on people at all levels is on the rise. Working supervisors and managers abound, doing much more than 20 percent nonexempt-type work with leaner staffs. Computers, rapid technological change, and increasing competition require a more flexible approach to current wage and hour regulations.

RAISES

Cost of Living Adjustment (COLA)

In order to help their employees keep up with inflation, some employers will grant annual cost of living increases. COLAs are most common during times of rapid inflation. The standard approach is to follow the current Consumer Price Index (CPI). The CPI is published by the Bureau of Labor Statistics and measures price changes for goods and services purchased by the average family. For example, if the CPI for a reporting year rose by 3 percent, all salaries would be raised by 3 percent.

Shift Differentials

Businesses opening up a second or even a third shift will grant pay differentials to attract and retain employees working hours after the standard workday. The differential can be provided as a percentage increase in pay, for example, 10 percent, or as extra cents per hour, for example, 50 cents added to the standard hourly rate.

Performance Raises

Getting a raise is a happy moment for most people, particularly when it is perceived as a fair reward for loyal service and good performance. Researchers claim that the long-term incentive value of traditional performance raises is questionable at best. Employees adjust quickly to the higher paycheck and the raise is soon forgotten. Most likely, it will not prompt them to work harder or smarter. Nonetheless, it is an important practice in retaining good workers and basic to the long-range success of any compensation program.

Depending on the organization or industry, companies take different approaches in timing performance raises. The more traditional approaches are described as follows:

- *The anniversary-date raise.* Employees are scheduled for a performance raise on or close to their anniversary date with the company. The advantage is that it spreads the administrative workload over the course of the year.
- *The calendar-year raise.* Employees get their raises at the beginning of the new year. Since the raises are not spread throughout the year, money must be available to cover the increases all at once.

- *The fiscal year raise.* As with calendar-year raises, employees receive their raises at one time but not at the beginning of the year. The company chooses a time of year that ties in with its budget cycle, commonly a midyear month such as June, July, or August.

Increase Amounts

The amount of money to allot for performance increases may depend on a variety of factors, ability to pay being the main one. Increase budgets at the time of this writing are averaging about 4 percent since inflation has been low and many companies are still downsizing staff and reducing payroll costs wherever they can. The amount an individual employee receives usually depends on his or her level of performance. For businesses with formal performance review systems an increase table can be developed; see Figure 2-6.

Controlling Payroll Costs

Besides pegging salary increases to level of performance, employers use other techniques designed to control payroll costs. The intent is to slow the process of moving up the salary range, thereby saving money and preventing employees from "maxing out" too soon.

Resist making exceptions to your established policies just to placate unhappy employees. Too many exceptions will erode the system and may result in morale problems. Unequal treatment can result in discrimination charges. The approach for these programs,

Figure 2-6   Increase Table

Overall Performance Rating	Increase (%)
Outstanding	7
Commendable	6
Competent	4 to 5
Acceptable	3
Unsatisfactory	0

like all other personnel operations, is fair and consistent application of your policies. If you do decide to make changes to existing programs, the changes should be well communicated in advance to your employees, preferably in writing. Provide an effective date for such changes, such as a forthcoming budget or calendar year.

Performance Review Cycles for Existing Employees

Extending the performance review cycle dates after the employee reaches a certain point in the salary range will help avoid the "maxing out" already described. For example, all employees stay on a 12-month review cycle until their salary reaches the midpoint of their range; then reviews go to a 15–18 month cycle.

More elaborate programs go beyond using range midpoints as the dividing line. Some organizations peg the raise cycle to quartiles within the ranges, while others use a specified percentage of the midpoint. Remember, if the system is too convoluted it is difficult to explain to employees. Again, they may not trust what they don't fully understand.

Performance Review Cycles for New Employees

When starting new workers at range minimums, many firms will place them on 3-, 6-, or 9-month review cycles until they reach a certain point within their range, often the midpoint. After it is reached, the cycle goes to 12 months or more. This is done to provide an added incentive to learn and adapt to the new job, as well as control costs.

Prorating Raises

Promotions elevate employees to higher level positions and salary range. One effective approach is to establish a standard promotional raise percentage given at the time of the promotion. If this amount does not bring an individual up to the minimum of the new range, an additional adjustment can be made at the time of promotion, or within six months if a wider gap exists.

When promoting someone before a scheduled performance raise, consider granting a prorated performance increase first, before adding the promotional raise amount.

The amount of a prorated raise depends on the number of months since the last regular review date. A method for calculating prorated increases is provided in Figure 2-7.

Figure 2-7   Prorated Promotional Increases

If the employee is on a 12-month annual performance review cycle and a
promotion occurs 7 months into that cycle, a prorated performance raise
may be granted in addition to the promotional increase.

Current salary: $14,000
3% annual performance increase = $420
$420 ÷ 12 = $35.00 per month
$35.00 × 7 = $245.00 prorated performance increase

ALTERNATIVES DURING LEAN TIMES

Hopefully your business is doing well, and expenses are being met
with little difficulty. If not, you have plenty of company. Tough times
have forced many businesses to cut back drastically in order to remain viable, and cutting personnel expense is a common practice
today. Even healthy, profitable companies are laying off employees
in order to streamline operations and look good to investors. Often
their stock will soar after a major layoff.

Before slashing payroll, however, have you considered all
other possible avenues for saving money? Can some programs be
curtailed or suspended until sales have improved? Have you gone
through the budget line items, cutting operating expenses as much
as possible?

Reducing Payroll Costs without Layoffs

If still faced with the need to cut payroll costs, consider using some
of the following approaches:

- *Reducing performance raise percentages.* Payroll performance
  budgets have been going down in recent years, averaging
  4 percent, just keeping up with inflation. Would cutting
  performance raises by a few percentage points ease the
  problem?

- *Extending the length of the performance review cycle.* Instead of a 12- or 15-month review cycle, can you extend it to 18 months or more to buy some relief?
- *Reducing the promotional raise percentage.*
- *Providing lump sum performance and/or promotional raises.* These lump sum amounts are not added to the base wage. The upside is you are not permanently raising salary costs, and the employees do get additional money in one payment rather than spread out in each paycheck throughout the year. The downside is you must have the funds available to pay lump sum amounts.
- *Placing a temporary freeze on raises.* Explain to your employees why this is necessary: that your first priority is to preserve the health of the company, including their jobs.
- *Wage reductions.* How much do you slice, and will you include your top people as well as yourself?

Attempt to be as fair and consistent as possible; there are no easy solutions. Equity issues with your employees are at stake. Be honest with them in explaining why these steps are necessary, and try to give them as much warning as possible.

Layoffs

Before implementing a staff layoff consider alternatives with a similar result, such as the following:

- *Hiring freeze.* Would a temporary hiring freeze be effective, allowing time for normal attrition to reduce payroll?
- *Part-time arrangements.* Would any full-time employees consider a change to part-time work to reduce payroll expense?
- *Unpaid leave of absence.* Would anyone volunteer for an extended leave of absence, without pay? If you provide health benefits, consider maintaining them during the leave. Someone may wish to have this time to take a course or spend time with children or aging parents.

- *Cut nonwage expenses.* Check again to see if you have done all you can to cut other expenses such as travel and entertainment, holiday parties, furniture and equipment purchases, supplies, and so forth.

The Criteria for Selection

If a layoff is inevitable, ensure that you have established fair and reasonable selection criteria based on sound business reasons. On what basis will the people be chosen: by seniority, by performance rating, by job duties? If by performance, do you have valid measurements to make a selection, such as performance review forms or documented individual production records?

The criteria used should be able to withstand close scrutiny in case of discrimination charges. List those employees initially selected by age, sex, race, and national origin to see if a pattern exists that could be construed as discriminatory by the Equal Employment Opportunity Commission (EEOC) or state human rights agency. Compare this information with the same information about your other employees. If a disproportionate number of females, older persons, or minority group members are represented, you'll want to take a second look to ensure that your original selection criteria will hold up under fire.

Caution is strongly recommended if employees on disability leave, or those just returned from disability leave, are on the layoff list. You may be vulnerable to a disability discrimination suit. You should have solid, business-necessity criteria. If there are any gray areas, you might be better off not including these folks! Apply the same caution with employees having recently incurred workers' compensation claims.

Rehire Policy

What are the chances for rehiring laid-off workers later on? Can you give them first preference if appropriate positions in the company open up? If so, can the same layoff criteria be used, but in *reverse* order, for those with good or better performance records?

Severance Pay

Will you provide severance or not? If you do, how much can you afford? One week, two weeks? Does your industry dictate a standard? How about one week for each year of service, with a limit? What about those employed less than a year? Whatever formula you choose, keep it simple so all employees will understand, and be consistent.

Employee Notification

Federal law dictates the layoff notification requirements for larger firms (those with over 100 employees) under the Worker Adjustment and Retraining Notification Act (WARN). (See Chapter 9, Legal Issues.) Whether or not WARN applies, you have two distinct categories of employees to notify: those laid off and the survivors. Timing is essential with both groups.

If WARN doesn't apply, how much notice will you give your people? Will you give them any notice at all? They may not be completely surprised, since rumors of pending layoffs often leak out. However, no one really wants to believe his or her name is on the layoff list. For security reasons, you may want them to leave right after notification, or at the end of the workday. For production reasons, they may be needed longer to finish or transfer remaining work to others. Will you pay them a bonus to do so? Which direction to take will depend on the workers involved, the nature of the work, and the morale within the company.

The compassionate approach would be to give the employees as much notice as possible before the paycheck runs out. This will allow them time to adjust and make future plans.

The Layoff Notification Meeting

If only a few employees are affected, you may choose to meet with each person privately at the end of the workday. Have individually addressed notification letters prepared in advance to be handed out to each person at this meeting. A sample layoff notification letter is provided in Figure 2-8.

Get right to the point. Explain the purpose of the meeting and give a brief overview of the business conditions that prompted the downsizing. Advise them of the effective date and severance pay arrangements. If they stand a chance of rehire when conditions improve, advise them, without making promises. Distribute the notification letters. These will be useful when they file for unemployment benefits and seek other positions.

Figure 2-8   Sample Layoff Notification Letter

Date:

John Smith
200 Magnolia Ave.
Atlanta, GA 30021

Dear John:

In order to address difficult economic and business conditions, I have made a thorough assessment of our financial obligations and commitments. Analysis of these commitments is now complete, and a decision has been reached to eliminate your position for economic reasons.

The effective date for this layoff is _____. You will receive _____ weeks' severance pay in accordance with our severance pay program, plus payment for any accrued but unused vacation time.

Information regarding your right to continue health benefits at your expense will be mailed to you shortly by certified letter.

This was a difficult yet necessary decision, and it was made only after all other alternatives were explored. We wish you well in your future career pursuits.

                              Sincerely,

                              A. J. Jones, Owner
cc: Personnel File

Simultaneously, someone else in authority should let surviving staff know what is going on, enabling you, not the grapevine, to control communications.

JOB GRADE STRUCTURES

Job Grade structures are traditionally found in midsize and larger organizations having multiple positions with similar salary ranges. For better control, these individual ranges are combined together according to levels of knowledge, skills, and responsibility. Hierarchical systems such as grades 1 through 10 (or higher) are common. Some firms have separate systems differentiating exempt and nonexempt jobs, or other classifications.

Under a graded system our Warehouse Supervisor could be classified as Warehouse Supervisor, grade 8 and share the same level as Accounts Payable Supervisor, grade 8. Other than supervising people, the jobs are very different but still share the same salary range. The ranges are often determined by market conditions as well as internal job evaluation techniques specific to the company.

Graded systems provide the visible rungs for the traditional career ladder. Recent trends are to reduce and flatten such structures, using fewer levels with wider range spans. Called broadbanding, the goal is to simplify compensation administration while allowing management more flexibility in assigning workers to different and/or higher-level job functions, while still remaining within their broadened salary range. For smaller firms with few position types, sophisticated job evaluation techniques will not be worth the time and expense. If you grow larger, however, some basic understanding of the principals of job evaluation may come in handy.

Job Evaluation Techniques

Job evaluation is a primary function of the compensation field. Its objective is to determine the relative worth of one job to another within and outside the organization by comparing the jobs and creating the job worth hierarchy. It's really a system of ranking jobs by their importance. Once the pecking order is defined, grade levels can be assigned to each position, from the highest to the lowest or vice versa. The goal is to achieve equity with the external market and within the company.

External Wage Equity

External equity is best achieved by staying in tune with the job market via wage and salary survey information, and adjusting your salaries and/or ranges where appropriate.

Your employees may not have access to sophisticated salary survey reports, but they do make informal wage comparisons with the outside market. They compare notes with friends, relatives, and customers who work for other companies, some within your industry. They may keep in contact with ex-employees who moved to a competitor for more money, and have copies of that competitor's wage ranges. They read newspapers and magazines, or pick up the latest scoop at a club meeting.

The process of determining market wages was covered earlier, using the benchmark position of Warehouse Supervisor. What do you do, however, if you can't find good benchmark equivalents for one of your new positions? A basic job evaluation technique called slotting may be in order.

Slotting involves comparing the new position duties against those jobs already in your structure and "slotting" it in where appropriate, using the closest salary range available, or adjusting an existing range to suit the new position. For example, if the new job is that of Assistant Supervisor, its salary range will fall below the salary range for Warehouse Supervisor, but may be higher than the Fork-Lift Operator salary range.

Internal Wage Equity

Internal equity issues arise when employees start to compare their salaries with other employees in your company. John feels he should be paid more than Fred because he feels his job is tougher or requires higher skills. The owner gets frustrated because each job is paid according to its respective market average, with Fred's being higher.

Small firms with few employees and job categories shouldn't have too much of a problem. With growth, however, equity issues multiply. The employer is now faced with maintaining both external (market) and internal equity. To achieve internal harmony a number of job evaluation techniques are available, including job ranking and quantitative methods.

Job ranking. Ranking is simple. All the jobs within the company are ranked according to their worth from highest to lowest in perceived value to the company. Owners can do this alone, or in concert with their key people for a cooperative effort. The ranking approach is not perfect because one must subjectively estimate where each job fits.

A subset of the ranking method is called *paired comparison.* This technique is used when many jobs must be ranked. On 3 × 5 cards, list each job title, one title to a card. Taking the first card, compare every other job to it, one at a time. Place a check on this first card every time it is ranked as *more* important than one of the other jobs. When finished with the first card, go to the next card, repeating the process until finished with all the cards. Then total the check marks on each card. The one with the most number of checks is the highest in the hierarchy; the rest follow in order of their value.

Quantitative methods of job evaluation. The ranking approach is limited in that whole jobs are compared with one another. Sometimes evaluators are unable to agree on which job is more valuable. More precise methods were needed, so quantitative methods were developed. These methods are more accurate, yet require extra time, effort, and expense to implement and maintain, particularly for smaller businesses. The following overview should put them into perspective.

The most common of the quantitative approaches is the point-factor method. It uses additional measuring criteria in order to make value comparisons. In compensation terms, these criteria are called *compensable factors.* The primary compensable factors are *skill, effort, responsibility,* and *working conditions.* Each factor is weighted according to the nature of the job. Then point values are assigned, lowest to highest, for each compensable factor. Figure 2-9 provides an illustration of this method.

The second column at the top of Figure 2-9 in the point-value scale repeats the weighting percentage numbers, then progresses arithmetically to higher values. The analyst chooses one point value in each row. The values chosen in each row are totaled to arrive at a *point score* for the position.

After each job is evaluated, each can be ranked by point values to create the job worth hierarchy. Different jobs with similar

Figure 2-9   Point-Factor Evaluation—Warehouse Supervisor

Compensable Factors	Weight (%)	Point-Value Scale $(35 \times 2 = 70; 70 \times 2 = 140,$ etc.)			
Skills	35	35	70	**140**	280
Effort	15	15	**30**	60	120
Responsibility	30	30	60	120	**240**
Working conditions	20	20	40	**80**	160

Compensable Factors	Points
Skill	140
Effort	30
Responsibility	240
Working Conditions	80
Total:	490

point value scores can be grouped together for the levels required in graded programs. New jobs are evaluated with the same system; the point score identifies the appropriate grade level with its assigned salary range.

The point-factor system can produce more accurate results than other, less sophisticated systems. It demands closer job analysis to assess the compensable factors and arrive at a score. Many point-factor systems go into even more depth, using subcategories within each main factor of skill, effort, responsibility, and working conditions as follows:

Skill

Education required
Manual dexterity
Knowledge

Effort

Mental effort
Concentration required
Physical effort

Responsibility

Financial
Supervisory
Quality

Working Conditions

Physical work hazards
Working environment
Level of stress

Gaming the System

Over time, the best evaluation systems can lose their effectiveness. It doesn't take long for employees to realize that more job points may translate into higher salary ranges. Some will insist that their job be reevaluated after assuming just a few additional work duties. Others will be reluctant to give up any duties lest their points be reduced, lowering their salary range.

Management and front-line supervisors are not immune to point inflation either. More points for jobs under their command may feather their own nest.

Communicating the Job Evaluation System

Before installing a job evaluation system, take the time to give everyone involved an overview of how the system works. Giving them the basics beforehand will save problems later on. The more complicated the system, the more time will be needed to educate and gain necessary support. What they don't understand, they mistrust. If the system is too mysterious, credibility will be lost.

Employees should be instructed that job evaluation techniques focus on the nature of the position, not the person currently in the job. Employees can easily get sidetracked with personality or performance issues, becoming disappointed when their job doesn't rate more points than they thought it would. After all, they may have worked very hard at it, being models for high performance and cooperation. When doing job evaluations remember that sometimes the person currently in the job will drive the position and it may be difficult to differentiate between actual job worth and the person performing the job.

Guidelines for Entrepreneurs and Small Business Owners

Compensation

When determining wages, keep in mind any nonwage employee benefits costs such as company insurance plans, paid sick days, vacation days, and so on. Using a total compensation view, you'll be able to keep wages in clearer perspective. Will you offset lower wages with employee health insurance? Or pay higher dollar wages with only a modest insurance package? Will you pay only the minimum wage with no insurance benefits at all?

Some key points to remember in this chapter are the following:

- Your base wage levels really depend on your ability to pay. No matter what the wage surveys indicate, you can't pay out money you don't have!
- Don't forget that you must match the employee's social security withholding tax with your own contribution when calculating payroll costs.
- Overtime costs can add up fast, so keep close track of the hours your people are working.
- Insist they get your approval before putting in overtime. Keep accurate time records!
- Ensure you have enough cash to meet quarterly payroll tax deposits! If cash flow is tight, pay these taxes, even if it means being behind in the rent.
- Employees in most small businesses are in the nonexempt category, so they are eligible for overtime pay. Wrestling with exempt/nonexempt status should not be a major problem. If you do have a worker who is on the borderline between these classifications and you're not sure which status to designate, take the safe route and pay overtime, at least until you can clear things up.

3

ORIENTATION
AND TRAINING

NEW EMPLOYEE ORIENTATION

Starting a new job is never easy; it's only natural for people to be nervous. For more timid souls, the experience can be frightening particularly when it's a first job. Employees remember their first day at work. They're definitely out of their comfort zone and require encouraging support for at least the first few days. Resist the pressure to put them right to work, sink or swim. First impressions have a lasting effect; few ever forget their early days on the job.

Orienting new people involves more planning and detail than might be expected. Developing a good program requires an empathetic mindset—the ability to put oneself into the new person's shoes. Things veteran workers know by heart may be a complete mystery to someone new. If you or a lead member of your staff will be doing the orientation, consider using some of the following tools to make it more effective:

- *The buddy system.* Assign an experienced coworker to show the new people the ropes for the first few days. Pick someone who is mature and friendly, with a good attitude toward the company. This is someone they'll go on breaks and eat lunch with and who will formally introduce coworkers. Using the buddy system is an excellent icebreaker.

- *Current table of organization.* Except in a really small firm, a current table of organization is quite useful in orienting new folks. Update it to include the new employee's name. The chart provides a snapshot of just where he or she fits into the structure and who everyone is including job functions and titles. Include everyone at all levels. Inexpensive software packages are now available that can produce organization charts in short order.

- *Photographs.* A picture is worth a thousand words so use one or more. Take photos of key management and supervisory staff, providing them to new members.

- *Directional plans.* Depending on business size and location, abbreviated floor plans showing unit locations, entrances, exits, restrooms, and so forth can be issued. It will save new hires the embarrassment and wasted time of getting lost.

- *Employee handbook.* A well-written handbook can save considerable time in answering common employee questions. Give them time to read it at work, or have them read it on their own time after hours.

- *Videos.* Rent or borrow a camcorder or bring one from home and tape an introductory message from the owner. Include introductions from other key people. Even though it's an amateur production you'll have fun doing it. A secondhand VCR for playing the tape shouldn't cost much.

- *Welcome notices.* Write a bulletin announcing the new employee. Provide his or her start date, position, and some background information. Notice should also be included in the company newsletter if you have one.

- *New-hire checklist.* Perhaps one of the most useful tools available is the new-hire checklist. With it you can ensure that all pertinent orientation items are covered. Give a copy to the employee as well. A second copy goes into the individual's main personnel file once orientation is completed.

Listed in alphabetical order are suggested subjects for your own new-hire checklist:

- Benefit enrollment completed
- Computer access arranged
- Confidentiality and proprietary statement
- Dress code regulations
- E-mail procedures
- Emergency evacuation procedures
- Employee handbook
- ID cards
- Job description given
- Locker assigned
- Name plates
- Office/desk supplies
- Office keys/card access
- Parking stickers
- Payroll schedule
- Safety equipment issued
- Safety procedures
- Security procedures
- Time clock/Time sheet procedures
- Wage withholding completed (both federal and state forms)
- Work manuals
- Work schedules
- Work tools

EMPLOYEE TRAINING

Too often, training is set aside because of other priorities. That's unfortunate because poorly trained workers make more mistakes, take longer to get up to speed, and are easily discouraged. Some may seek direction from your less effective workers, absorbing bad habits. Training your employees at critical points in your operation takes effort and imagination but the payoffs are worthwhile. Unless you do it yourself, training should be assigned to the most experienced, mature person you have on staff.

Training as Corrective Action

Training can be part of the corrective action process when someone is not meeting standards. Consider it one more option in your efforts to give the employee every opportunity to improve. With new employees, failure to successfully complete the initial training program may result in termination or, at best, assignment to another available job.

Training and Equal Employment Opportunity

Training, like salary, raises, promotions, transfers, and terminations, is considered a condition of employment by the Equal Employment Opportunity Commission (EEOC). Keep good records of who is trained, when, and on what subjects. Opportunities for training should be unbiased, fair, and nondiscriminatory. By keeping good records you can monitor whether or not people in protected classes are receiving equal training opportunities and take corrective action when needed.

Training and the Occupational Safety and Health Administration

The federal Occupational Safety and Health Administration (OSHA) may request to audit your training records, particularly if safety training is performed. If an accident investigation is held, well-documented safety training records will support your good faith training efforts to prevent accidents.

Training as a Reward

Training can be an effective motivation tool, particularly when the employee has the opportunity to apply the new training once back on the job.

Training Outlines

In-house training can be made more effective by writing a simple training outline. Use it as a road map for training in an organized, effective fashion. Preparing an outline gives you an opportunity to review and revise existing procedures. It can be reused to train future workers, providing consistency.

Training outlines come in a variety of formats. A sample outline is shown in Figure 3-1, and an explanation of each section of the form is provided.

Training Objectives

Take the time to outline specific training objectives for the job in question. Focus on the major job functions. You don't have to train for all aspects of a specific job. Stick to the basics, letting the employee pick up the minor details later on.

Adjust your objectives to the person being trained. Some employees may already have job knowledge, others may need more time to learn, particularly those who have a disability. Share the training objectives with the trainees. They'll appreciate knowing just what is expected of them, often reducing their anxiety and yours.

The following are some examples of training objectives:

Upon completion of this lesson, the employee will be able to produce 50 widgets per hour on the Alpha milling machine with less than a 2-percent error rate.

Upon completion of training, the trainee will be able to produce five sample business letters accurately utilizing the word processing macros listed below.

At the end of this module, the operator will be able to accurately demonstrate the following functions on our telephone communications system: four call transfers, three conference calls including four participants, set up and recording of two voice mail messages.

Lesson Plan

Cluster key tasks to be learned into a logical sequence using a building block approach. Training should proceed one step at a time. Limit each task to 10 or 15 minutes, followed by time for the trainee to demonstrate mastery and confidence. Allow time for practice before moving on to the next segment. Be sure to provide encouragement along the way.

Time is critical when conducting training sessions. It is very easy to fall behind schedule, so indicate in the plan the starting times for each segment. Keep close track of your schedule.

Figure 3-1   Training Outline

Training Outline

Date:_____

Subject:_____   Employee Name:_____

Training Objectives: (Specify exactly what the trainee is to know, demonstrate, or perform once trained. How will results be measured?)

Upon completion of this training the employee will be able to do the following:

1. _____
   _____
   _____

2. _____
   _____
   _____

3. _____
   _____
   _____

4. _____
   _____
   _____

5. _____
   _____
   _____

6. _____
   _____
   _____

-1-

(continued)

Figure 3-1   *Continued*

Lesson Plan: (Outline the logical steps required to deliver this training. Indicate the time each step will start. Include where slides, videos, flip chart illustrations, or other support material will be presented.)

Session I   Time
1._____   _____
2._____   _____
3._____   _____
4._____   _____

Session II
1._____   _____
2._____   _____
3._____   _____
4._____   _____

Session III
1._____   _____
2._____   _____
3._____   _____
4._____   _____

Session IV
1._____   _____
2._____   _____
3._____   _____
4._____   _____

Session V
1._____   _____
2._____   _____
3._____   _____
4._____   _____

Visual Aids: (Identify what types of visual aids will be required to complete this training.)

_____
_____
_____

Support Materials: (Identify handbooks, guide sheets, sample work, and other items needed to support this lesson.)

_____
_____

-2-

Practice! Practice! Practice! Current learning theory indicates that practicing a task at least three times enhances retention. Also, adults learn and retain more if given an opportunity to apply their skills and experience, so provide for active participation whenever possible.

Visual Aids

We live in a time when we are all bombarded with special effects imagery: television, wide-screen movies, video games, and subliminal advertising. Instructors relying on their own personality to deliver training lessons without visual aids do so at their own peril. Trainees easily become bored, particularly with straight lectures. Effective trainers integrate appropriate visual material to supplement verbal instructions and discussions. Commonly used tools include the following:

- *Overhead projectors.* Key points can be introduced first on an overhead transparency (also called overheads), then discussed in order, one by one. Timed properly, instructors use overheads to focus a group's attention on material, reinforcing verbal delivery. When using overhead projectors always have a spare bulb handy!
- *Charts, graphs, and diagrams.* With modern software, smaller firms can produce first-rate graphic materials that just a few years ago were reserved for big-dollar companies. Printed graphics can be transferred to transparency sheets fed through a photocopier and used on overhead projectors.
- *Flip charts.* This is another effective means of supplementing instruction. Consider having at least two around the workplace since they are always in demand. Use different colored markers to illustrate instructional material. Flip charts are a must for encouraging student participation. Use one chart to highlight your instructions, a second one to record trainee responses to questions.
- *Videocassette recorder.* Videotapes are another excellent training tool, particularly when providing prepackaged supervisory training programs. Many of these programs use videotapes to demonstrate effective interviews, corrective action sessions, and performance discussions.

Support Materials

Support materials include such things as work checklists and machine operating instructions. Lists defining industry terms, abbreviations, and acronyms can be very useful. Printed copies of the transparencies presented on your overhead projector or flip charts may be helpful.

After-Hours Training

If training during normal business hours is impractical, consider evening sessions. Ensure that employees have enough advance notice, particularly those who must make alternative child care arrangements. Have dinner brought in—perhaps pizza? Let them dress informally. Weekend sessions are another alternative. Remember, any mandatory training at the company's request may require overtime pay for nonexempt staff.

Learn-over-Lunch Programs

Learning over lunch can be an excellent way to provide employees with helpful information. Attendance is voluntary and employees bring their own lunch. Guest speakers can be brought in for lunchtime lectures on general interest subjects. For a reasonable fee, many local health providers offer programs on a variety of subjects such as cancer prevention, exercise, diet, and stress management. Also popular are lectures on personal and home security conducted by local law enforcement agencies.

Learn-over-lunch programs are particularly effective when weather conditions keep employees indoors during lunch hours. They provide a nice break from the daily work routine.

Training Certificates

Award training certificates with the company logo acknowledging successful completion of training courses. Place a copy in the employee's personnel file.

Outside Training

One- and two-day workshops covering administrative assistant skills, planning, legal compliance, customer service, and a host of other subjects applicable to most businesses are available. Local colleges, business and trade associations, and commercial training companies offer a diversity of programs.

Larger businesses in your area may have established in-house training units. Perhaps they can be persuaded to include some of your staff members in their programs or allow one of their trainers to conduct sessions at your location, both for a reasonable fee. It will help reduce their overhead costs and they can take credit for turning their training unit into a profit center for their organization.

Outside Supervisory Training

Supervisory training should be a priority, particularly for those new to management and supervision. Untrained supervisors can easily expose your company to lawsuits, so focus on programs that will help them avoid trouble when dealing with their employees, such as workshops on civil rights laws, wage and hour regulations, fair employment practices, disciplinary action procedures, and dealing with difficult people.

Independent trainers may be available to conduct sessions on a contract basis. Call the local chapter of the American Society of Training and Development (ASTD) for sources. Trainers of all categories often hold ASTD membership. For more information, write to the American Society for Training and Development, Suite 305, 600 Maryland Avenue S.W., Washington, DC 20024.

Guidelines for Entrepreneurs and Small Business Owners

Orientation and Training

As an entrepreneur, most likely you will enter new situations with minimal trepidation. The new and unknown is a challenge. To most people, however, change is both scary and difficult. This is especially true for folks starting a new job. Many will resist asking questions, wishing to not appear stupid or foolish. This is all the more reason for effective orientation and training as soon as new employees arrive for work.

- Sink or swim is a common approach to new workers, but it usually costs business owners more money than the orientation and training approach. Workers without direction can make costly mistakes, even become a danger to themselves and the business if they are not shown proper techniques and procedures. The customer is usually the first to know.
- Carve out the time required to orient new people as soon as they arrive for work. If Monday is too busy a day, start them on Tuesday or even midweek when you do have the time.
- Never assume new people will be self-starters or quick studies during their first week at work. Some very competent people must be primed with initial guidance and instruction in the early days. If properly trained, their self-confidence and competence will evolve much faster as they master their new job.
- Training need not be sophisticated or expensive. A small business owner can do wonders just by going over duties and responsibilities with a new person in an organized, methodical fashion. Even a handwritten checklist is effective.
- Training takes a lot of patience. This trait is not paramount in entrepreneurs anxious to get things

(continued)

Continued

moving—fast! Perhaps you can delegate most training to a senior person who has a flair for instructing others.

- If you add a supervisor, supervisory training is strongly recommended. Most people are not born supervisors. Most get to the supervisory level because of education, competence in their field, hard work, seniority, loyalty to the owner, or politics, but not usually because they are skilled in handling subordinates. Focus supervisory training on equal opportunity and other employment laws. Spend your money in this area because it's where an untrained supervisor can cause you the most damage.

4

WORKPLACE POLICIES AND PROCEDURES

With staff growth, the number and variety of personnel issues increase. Entrepreneurs no longer have time to handle all questions personally. The need for written policies becomes apparent. Well-written policies and procedures can be a valuable communications tool for employees. They communicate the ground rules ahead of time, providing an important framework for day-to-day operations. If you don't have time to write them yourself perhaps your lead person could start the process.

Once put to print, however, the obligation to enforce and apply policies and procedures consistently increases. Policy distribution is not without its risks. Your attorney should review all policies before distribution to look for language that could be misinterpreted as implying promises or contracts not intended by the company, or text incompatible with current employment legislation.

Policies common to many types of companies are also available in prewritten form. One published source is called *Prewritten*

Personnel Policies by Business and Legal Reports. Their toll-free telephone number is 800-727-5257. The cost is about $200. Personnel policy manuals are also being produced on computer disk and are available for less than $100 in the software section of some computer and office supply stores.

Developing and communicating employee policy is more art than science. A balance must be struck between depth of detail and need for flexibility. Printing all policies and procedures is overkill. Some should not be put in writing.

The following alphabetical list includes policies and procedures common to most businesses. Many should be put in writing. Where appropriate, sample text is given in *italic* to use as a reference source when writing your own versions. Policies and procedures covered in this chapter include the following:

- Attendance and punctuality
- Bulletin boards
- Business ethics
- Conduct
- Confidential and proprietary information
- Dress code
- EEOC statements
- Employee personnel files
- Employee problem resolution
- Job openings
- Loans and pay advances
- Marriage between coworkers
- Overtime
- Performance appraisal
- Personal property
- Personal telephone calls and mail
- Reemployment
- Resignations
- Salary administration
- Salary increases
- Sexual harassment
- Smoking
- Solicitation

ATTENDANCE AND PUNCTUALITY

Absence and lateness of employees can hurt production, placing additional burdens on other employees. Employees are expected to be in and ready to work on time.

If you expect to be late or absent, notify your supervisor as soon as possible. If you are absent more than one day, call in daily unless otherwise notified.

A written doctor's note is required if you are out _____ or more consecutive workdays due to illness, injury, or other disability.

BULLETIN BOARDS

Bulletin boards are located within the work areas to communicate information to our staff. They are for company use and management is responsible for the posting of all information. Items may include job openings, information about company-sponsored events and activities, and legally required notices.

BUSINESS ETHICS

(_____ , Inc.) is committed to conducting its business according to the highest legal, moral, and ethical standards. As an employee of the company we expect you to deal honestly and fairly with customers, suppliers, and coworkers. By maintaining these standards, we enhance the good name and reputation our company has earned throughout the community.

CONDUCT

We all have obligations to the company and our coworkers regarding our personal conduct. The following behaviors create work disturbances and dangerous or undesirable working conditions and are not permitted:

- *Drinking alcohol. Anyone appearing to be under the influence of alcohol will not be allowed to work.*

- *Abusive behavior including fighting and bad language is not permitted.*
- *The sale, use, or possession of illegal drugs or controlled substances is not permitted on company premises.*

CONFIDENTIAL AND PROPRIETARY INFORMATION

Owners may require employees to read and/or sign statements acknowledging their understanding of policies regarding the unauthorized or inappropriate disclosure of information considered confidential or owned by the company (proprietary). Signed copies of these statements are placed within the personnel file. In addition, the text of these statements may be incorporated within employee handbooks as well. Work with your attorney in developing the appropriate text.

DRESS CODE

The trend toward casual dress in the workplace continues to grow in popularity. It's more comfortable and employees can save on dry-cleaning costs. Many feel more relaxed and productive on the job. Also, with the emphasis on teamwork and worker empowerment, casual dress helps blur distinctions between management and workers.

All employees are required to dress neatly and appropriately while at work. Consult with your supervisor on the dress code requirements for your area.

Entrepreneurs should have more flexibility on this subject. Again, how you deal with this issue will depend on the nature of your business and the image you wish to project to customers and/or competitors. Some firms have a casual dress day once each week, others every day. Certain casual days may be canceled if outside VIPs will be touring the facilities. Casual dress may be just for employees working in internal areas where there is little or no customer contact. Front office receptionists and customer service and sales people might be excluded.

If you choose a casual dress policy, specify what is considered casual wear. Everyone should be clean and well groomed. Will you permit blue jeans or other types of jeans? How about sweat shirts and pants, or nylon exercise suits? Are shorts and halter tops prohibited? Shower slippers? Shoes with no socks? It's surprising what some people will wear to work. Why not ask your employees to draw up a list of what they think is acceptable and present it for your review.

EEOC STATEMENTS

Organizations frequently include a statement regarding policy on equal opportunity employment.

It is the policy of _____ , Inc. to treat all applicants and employees without regard to race, color, religion, sex, national origin, age, physical or mental handicap or disability, marital status, or status as a Vietnam-era veteran or disabled veteran.

If you feel you have been discriminated against by anyone in the company, report it to your supervisor. Your report will be handled confidentially.

EMPLOYEE PERSONNEL FILES

Personnel files are maintained for all employees within the company. Included are employment applications, résumés, performance appraisals, training records, and other documents related to employment.

The personnel files are kept confidential with access given to only those persons with a valid need to know. You can review your own file and if you see incorrect information please request that the appropriate changes be made. Help us keep your file up-to-date by promptly notifying us of any changes to your personal status such as marriage, divorce, change of address and telephone number, and emergency contact person.

Information in your file will be released to outside parties only when the company responds to duly authorized requests from legal agencies, such as summonses, subpoenas, and judicial orders, or with written permission from you.

EMPLOYEE PROBLEM RESOLUTION

Employees will have work-related and other problems requiring a solution. Recognizing this fact in writing and outlining the steps to take when problems arise will help solve them faster.

Please inform your supervisor of any problems or concerns related to work. Many problems can be resolved with your supervisor. If not, the company's employee problem resolution process should be used as follows:

- *First step. Give your supervisor the opportunity to resolve the issue first. If you don't feel comfortable with that person, go to your manager. The management person will try to resolve the issue at this stage.*
- *Second step. If the matter is not resolved at the first step, go to the next level of management. The person receiving your complaint at this level will attempt to resolve it.*
- *Last step. If you are not satisfied with the answer you get at the second step you can appeal the decision to the owner.*

JOB OPENINGS

As appropriate positions become available, the company may choose to post them in order to give employees an opportunity to apply and be considered as internal candidates. These positions will be posted from time to time on company bulletin boards and will outline required qualifications.

LOANS AND PAY ADVANCES

Sooner or later an employee is going to ask for a loan, often in terms of an advance on future pay. How will you respond?

Lending money to employees is risky business. It may jeopardize relationships because the company becomes the employee's creditor. Resentment can easily set in, particularly if repayment becomes a problem. If the employee should leave the company, you may never recover the money.

Pay advances create similar problems, although fewer dollars may be involved. When paid back in installments, advances add additional administrative expense in processing payroll. Also, you become vulnerable to other employees needing money. Where do you draw the line?

Loan provisions in a company-sponsored 401(k) plan may reduce loan requests. The employee borrows from his or her own account. However, many workers don't participate in savings plans.

MARRIAGE BETWEEN COWORKERS

When two employees marry, it is ideal if you can ensure that one spouse does not report directly to the other. If the firm is big enough, consider keeping them in separate units. If neither of these situations is practical and you decide one must leave the company, check your state laws, as some have passed legislation prohibiting termination due to marriage. (More often than not it was the wife who had to do the leaving!) You may also be accused of discriminating against employees on the basis of their marital status.

OVERTIME

Overtime work is sometimes necessary to meet workload requirements. When asked to work overtime, the company expects you to do so if at all possible. Your supervisor will try to give you advance notice and to accommodate your personal needs and commitments should conflicts arise.

If you are in a job properly classified as nonexempt, you will receive overtime compensation in accordance with provisions of the Fair Labor Standards Act (FLSA). Employees who are classified as exempt are not eligible for overtime compensation. Your job is considered exempt or nonexempt based on duties, responsibilities, and base salary. Check with your supervisor to find out which classification applies to you.

PERFORMANCE APPRAISAL

Under our performance appraisal program you and your supervisor will periodically sit down and formally review your work performance. The appraisal can be useful in helping you understand your duties and responsibilities and how well you have been performing. It can also assist you and your supervisor in identifying appropriate training and/or developmental activities to help you improve performance or acquire new skills.

PERSONAL PROPERTY

You have a responsibility to be careful of your personal belongings, as damage or theft can occur. You should avoid bringing to work large sums of cash or articles that are expensive or have substantial personal value. If something is missing or damaged on company premises, promptly report this to your supervisor.

PERSONAL TELEPHONE CALLS AND MAIL

Some employees will consider the company postage meter to be an added benefit and use it to mail out their holiday greeting cards, monthly personal bill payments, and so forth. Some will use the company address for personal mail such as personal bills the employee does not wish a spouse or other family member to see at their home address. You may encounter a personal side business run by an employee, with transactions coming through company mail. You can help stop these practices before they begin by prohibiting them in writing.

To control personal telephone calls, circulate the monthly telephone toll statements to your employees (if your phone system can identify long distance charges by extension). When employees know that phone charges are being monitored, abuses should diminish.

Because of the heavy volume handled by the company's mail and telephone systems, you should not use these services for your personal needs. At most locations, public telephones are nearby and convenient for the occasional personal call you may need to make. Naturally, in the event of an emergency, you may use your office telephone to make or receive calls. You'll be expected to reimburse the company for excessive personal use of the office telephone.

REEMPLOYMENT

Former employees may be considered for rehire if they meet the following conditions:

- *They submit a written application.*
- *They meet the requirements of the open position.*
- *They were in good standing at the time of termination.*

RESIGNATIONS

Resignations should be in writing.

Employment with _____ , Inc. has always been subject to termination by the company or the employee at any time. If you plan to resign, give a signed, written notice to your supervisor at least two weeks before you leave. This will help ensure that the company has enough time to find a replacement or assign your work to others.

Sometimes you'll be pleased when a particular employee resigns. When this happens you may wish to give written acknowledgment and acceptance of the resignation, then proceed quickly to recruit a replacement before this person changes his or her mind. Sometimes an employee will attempt to rescind a resignation. An acceptance memo from the company helps close the door.

Voluntary Resignation Notice

Traditionally, two weeks is the standard notice for resignation. But employees are not obligated to give notice unless they are under some sort of contract or union agreement that requires it. If an employee is leaving for a position with a competitor and security is an issue, you may decide to ask that person to leave immediately. However, since he or she offered notice, it is recommended that you pay for the notice period. This may not be appropriate if early departure makes possible an earlier start date with the new employer. Collecting two paychecks for the same period is not fair to you or the new employer.

Counteroffers

Making counteroffers to resigning employees is not recommended. Statistics have shown that most employees who accept counteroffers will leave anyway within six months to a year. In the meantime, you pay them more money.

Abandonment of Position

Abandonment of position occurs when the employee disappears with no notice and no calls. Attempts to reach the employee at home or through coworkers prove fruitless. Wait at least a week, then send a letter to his or her last known address advising that the company has assumed that he or she has abandoned the position, and a resignation will be processed effective as of the last day worked. Keep any undeliverable mail returned by the post office in that person's personnel file as proof of your efforts to communicate.

SALARY ADMINISTRATION

The amount you are paid while you work at _____ , Inc. is based on the job you hold, the knowledge, skills, and experience you bring to the job, and the market rate for the position. Salary ranges are established based on comparisons with other jobs in the company and surveys of other company salaries. These ranges are reviewed periodically and revised when necessary to remain competitive.

SALARY INCREASES

Our company provides different types of salary increases. You will be regularly considered for a pay increase. The timing and amount depend on your latest performance review, your level of performance, and where your current salary falls within your salary range. If you receive a promotion, you may be eligible for an additional promotional increase.

SEXUAL HARASSMENT

Sexual harassment is a hot topic in the media today. Making company policy known on this issue is a wise idea, so many firms include some sort of statement in their handbook. The statement that follows directs employees who believe they have been sexually harassed to go to their manager or supervisor, giving the company the opportunity to settle the matter internally, hopefully avoiding litigation and publicity.

Sexual harassment is a violation of company policy. Unwelcome sexual advances, requests for sexual favors, and other verbal or physical conduct of a sexual nature constitute sexual harassment when one or more of the following applies:

- *Submission to the conduct is made to be a condition for keeping your job.*
- *Submission to or rejection of the conduct is used as the basis for other employment decisions affecting your job.*
- *The harassment substantially interferes with an employee's work performance or creates an intimidating, hostile, or offensive work environment.*

If you want to report an incident in which you feel sexual harassment may be occurring or may have occurred, advise your supervisor as soon as possible. Your report will be handled confidentially.

SMOKING

The trend toward restricting or banning smoking in the workplace is accelerating. Government agencies, both federal and state, and the larger corporations have led this trend. The antismoking movement is strong and nonsmokers are becoming increasingly adamant about the issue. The backlash by smokers can be severe, creating bitterness and hard feelings at work. It can be a very sensitive issue, particularly when you must restrict some of your better employees. The potential for liability lawsuits will increase for employers.

There are a variety of smoking policy alternatives, as described in the following sections.

Segregate Smokers from Nonsmokers

Continue to allow smoking but segregate the smokers from the nonsmokers in the work unit. This may help, but the smoke still circulates through the air ducts to the nonsmokers, although it is less visible.

Smoking Room

Provide a separate smoke break room for smokers. The only truly effective ones have separate ventilation systems that exhaust the smoke outside the building. This could be expensive or prohibited by the landlord.

Stop Smoking Programs

Arrange for a number of stop smoking programs for those who wish to quit entirely. Many smokers really want to quit and will see this ban as an opportunity to do so. The American Lung Association is one source of information and help. Stop smoking sessions can be held at your workplace during or after hours; off-site group sessions are available at low cost. More expensive alternatives such as the nicotine patch or hypnosis are available. Whatever programs you offer, it is recommended that you require that the employee share in their cost; it increases commitment.

Complete Smoking Ban

The complete ban may prove to be the only practical solution. Unless you own your facilities you may not have a choice, as some landlords have begun to ban smoking completely, not just in the lobbies, rest rooms, and elevators. If you opt for a complete ban the following should be done to ensure a smoother transition:

- Give the employees plenty of advance notice, for example, three to six months before the ban will go into effect.
- Clearly specify the effective date and hold to it. This will give your smokers plenty of time to adjust and perhaps even quit smoking. It should also pacify your more strident antismoking employees.
- Advise all job applicants that there will be no smoking in the workplace. Put it in your employment ads as well.
- Ask your nonsmokers to be supportive during this transition. They should expect their coworkers to be nervous, tense, and sometimes short-tempered.

- Consider smoke breaks outside the workplace once the ban is in effect. Heavy smokers who can't quit will need one. Expect complaints however; nonsmokers may want equal break time.
- Remember to call your insurer if you are providing health benefits. You may be eligible for a premium discount if there is no smoking in your workplace.
- Ensure that everyone understands that the smoking ban applies to not only their regular workplace but also to any company meetings you hold at an off-site facility such as a hotel conference room.

Caution: Some companies have decided to screen out smokers in the hiring process. Some state and local governments have passed laws to protect smokers from discrimination.

SOLICITATION

People sell things at the workplace, including magazines, candy, holiday greeting cards and wrapping paper, raffle tickets, books, and cookies, and there are charity drives, and so forth. Sales flyers are placed on desks, pinned to bulletin boards and partitions, and pasted to walls, doors, computer screens, and other equipment.

Left unchecked these practices can become a nuisance to coworkers, particularly if they are short of cash. People don't like being pressured to buy something they may not want or contribute to a cause or charity to which they don't subscribe. If solicitation is becoming a problem in your firm, consider a written solicitation policy covering the following areas:

1. *Outside Solicitors.* Outsiders should never be permitted access to the workplace to solicit employees. Good security alone dictates their restriction. Train your receptionists to stop them at the door or foyer, politely explaining company policy and refusing to accept sample merchandise, stacks of flyers, catalogs, or order forms.
2. *Social Club.* Consider channeling employee solicitation through the employee social committee or activities club if you have one. Social committees will sponsor a variety of

activities and services for employees. They publicize their activities through established procedures and encourage participation on a voluntary basis.

3. *Company Bulletin Boards.* Maintain bulletin boards only for company-sponsored communications such as job openings, legally required notices, information about scheduled company events (including employee social committee activities), or other appropriate management or employee information. To maintain better control, the best approach is to spend the extra money and install bulletin boards with glass doors that lock.

Issue a written no solicitation policy such as the following: *Unless you are involved in the coordination of company-sponsored activities, you may not solicit or distribute literature on company premises during your working time or during the working time of others. You may not distribute literature in working areas at any time. Literature may not be strewn or discarded on company property. People who are not employed by our company are not permitted to solicit or distribute literature on company property at any time.*

Note: Consistent application of a no solicitation policy is particularly important for those businesses that may be vulnerable to union organizing campaigns either now or when they grow to a larger, more lucrative size.

Guidelines for Entrepreneurs
and Small Business Owners

Workplace Policies and Procedures

Written policies and procedures convey the idea of bureaucracy to many entrepreneurs. Their instincts tell them not to be
restricted by rules and regulations. Too much in writing can become restrictive or lose its impact as a result of overkill. Few
people want to have a rule book thrown at them, particularly in
a smaller business in which flexibility is essential for survival.
Too few policies or none at all can create confusion and misun-
derstanding with employees. Most will appreciate knowing
the ground rules and having them in writing. The key is to
strike the right balance between the two extremes. Some point-
ers when addressing this task include the following:

- Even a small firm should have some written policies.
  The absolute minimum should include written guide-
  lines in areas that can cause legal problems for employers of all sizes.
  — Equal employment opportunity statements
  — Employee problem resolution procedures
  — Sexual harassment policy
  — Attendance policy
- Whenever you put personnel policies in writing, have
  your attorney edit them before distribution.
- When policies and procedures are published, the
  owner has an obligation to follow them consistently
  and fairly. Companies do get sued by their employees
  and former employees for not following their own
  rules. In effect, they get hit over the head with their
  own policy manual.
- If you aren't up to the necessary diligence and follow
  through, you may be better off not having written
  policies at all.

5

PERFORMANCE EVALUATION

Employees fortunate enough to work for more communicative owners have a pretty good idea how well they're performing long before the scheduled performance review. They get their cues from frequent interactions with their bosses who praise, encourage, and guide them as work is accomplished. Constant feedback, given in an atmosphere of trust and mutual respect, improves morale and productivity. The formal performance review confirms and clarifies what the employee already knows!

The primary reason for formal reviews is to provide feedback on just how well people are doing their jobs. A scheduled review ensures this is accomplished. At its best, it enables both owner and worker to further clarify performance results and future expectations.

Written reviews serve other important purposes such as the following:

- Documentation on which to base promotions, raises, or bonuses

- Assessment of training and/or educational opportunities
- Documentation to support terminations, layoffs, or demotions if challenged in court

Conducting performance reviews is not high on an entrepreneur's to do list. Procrastination or outright avoidance is common. Unfortunately, reviews are often given at the last minute, in haste. Let's get this over with! Some reasons for this are the following:

- The small business owner may lack the training and/or experience required to conduct an effective performance review. The best performance systems won't work unless employees have a reasonable level of trust and respect for their boss.
- It is human nature for people to wish to be liked. Some bosses are reluctant to correct subordinates because they fear loss of worker support.
- Work standards may not exist, making it difficult to measure performance objectively.
- The review system may be inappropriate or too sophisticated for small operations.

Performance evaluation programs require support from the business owner in order to be effective. Some entrepreneurs have spent small fortunes on the development and installation of state-of-the-art evaluation systems only to let them drift because, after the initial enthusiasm was over, focus shifted to another priority and efforts were not sustained. If you decide to implement your own program, be ready for the effort required to keep it afloat.

TYPES OF PERFORMANCE EVALUATION FORMS

Over the last two decades a variety of approaches have been developed to measure employee performance. Since we are measuring people, there is no one perfect technique. This chapter discusses the more popular form designs and their advantages and disadvantages. Ready-to-use samples are provided. Key ingredients are provided to help you design your own forms to suit your particular business and management style.

The following types of forms are covered in this section:

- Traditional performance review forms
- Job-specific forms
- Management by objective forms
- Combination forms

Traditional Performance Evaluation Forms

Traditional performance evaluation forms come in a wide variety of designs, yet they share one thing in common: they use personality traits to measure performance. Examples of traits are cooperativeness, ability to handle stress, and flexibility. Traditional forms are common and easy to use. The form, with its descriptive phrases, leads the evaluator through the review process.

The Upside
Since they are so general, the traditional forms can be used for a wide variety of positions. Most of the personality traits (called performance factors) can be applied to any job since they are not job specific. These forms do not become out of date and minimal training and education are required to complete them.

The Downside
The disadvantage of the traditional form is that it focuses on personality traits rather than the job itself. The term cooperativeness may mean one thing to the entrepreneur, another to the employee. When pressed to defend the rating, the reviewer is often at a loss. These forms evaluate employees at the end of the review period. Most employees are flying blind up to that point, not really knowing how they're performing. See Figure 5-1 for a sample traditional form.

Narrative Forms
Some firms do not assign rating levels when doing evaluations. They use narrative comments instead to indicate performance. The traditional form in Figure 5-2 does not have provision for an overall rating level, but leaves room for comments under each rating factor.

Figure 5-1 Traditional Performance Review Form

EMPLOYEE PERFORMANCE RATING

Employee Name: Last   First   Middle   Department:_____

Position   Employment Date:

PERFORMANCE FACTORS
(Circle one in each category.)

Quality	**What is the quality of this employee's work?**
	Does extremely high quality work 5
	Work quality is usually above required standards 4
	Meets required standards...3
	Sometimes below standards 2
	Unsatisfactory 1
Quantity	**Does the employee meet the quantity standards for the position?**
	Exceptionally high producer 5
	Quantity is usually above standards 4
	Meets quantity standards...3
	Sometimes below standards 2
	Unsatisfactory 1
Teamwork	**Is the employee a team worker?**
	Outstanding team worker 5
	Works very well with others 4
	Teamwork ability meets required level to perform the job 3
	Is not always cooperative...2
	Unsatisfactory 1
Dependability	**How dependable is this employee?**
	Extremely reliable 5
	Very reliable, requires little supervision 4
	Reliable, requires average supervision.......................................3
	Requires above-average supervision 2
	Unsatisfactory 1

Overall   5. Outstanding _____   3. Competent _____
Rating   4. Commendable _____   2. Acceptable _____   1. Unsatisfactory _____

Comments: (Include any pertinent points not covered above, such as outstanding traits or areas for improvement. Use other side of page if necessary.)

Employee Comments: (Use other side of page if necessary.)

Employee Signature _____ Date _____
(I have read this evaluation.)

Supervisor Signature _____ Date _____

Figure 5-2   Narrative Performance Review Form

EMPLOYEE PERFORMANCE RATING

Employee Name:	Last	First	Middle	Department:_____

Position   Employment Date:

RATING FACTORS

Quality   Up to standards? Consider accuracy, neatness, and general efficiency.

_____

_____

Quantity   Does quantity of work measure up to standards? Consult production
                          records.

_____

_____

Cooperativeness   Is employee a team worker? Willing to assume share of work?
                          Does employee get along with others?

_____

_____

Dependability   How conscientiously are responsibilities carried out?

_____

_____

Adaptability   What ability is evidenced in adjusting to changing work or conditions?

_____

_____

Other: (Include any pertinent points not covered above, such as outstanding traits, areas for
improvement. Use other side of page if necessary.)

_____

Employee Comments: (Use other side of page if necessary.)

Employee Signature _____   Date _____
                          (I have read this evaluation.)

Supervisor Signature _____   Date _____

Job-Specific Forms

Job-specific evaluation forms measure actual job duties and responsibilities rather than general personality. See Figure 5-3 for a sample.

- *Duties* are specific tasks making up the job, which must be performed on a daily basis. Examples are answering telephones, unloading trucks, operating equipment, word processing, data entry on a computer, operating a lathe, and so on.
- *Responsibilities* are combinations of duties leading to an end result or product. Specific examples are: Responsible for delivering all interoffice mail by 10:00 A.M. daily; Balance petty cash transactions daily by 4:00 P.M.; Process incoming catalog orders within two working days.

You can construct these forms yourself by selecting the most important duties and responsibilities from your job descriptions as well as consulting employees doing the work. Obtaining employee feedback and cooperation enhances the form's credibility. Quantity and quality standards can be incorporated if you have actual targets to attain.

The Upside
The advantage of this style of form is that the factors measured are more closely linked to the job than to personality traits. Both supervisor and employee know in advance what is being measured.

The Downside
The downside is that it takes time and effort to evaluate each job, prioritize duties and responsibilities, set standards, and evaluate compliance. Also, stability must exist in the workplace. This is not always achievable if the staff is running from one priority to another.

Management by Objectives (MBO) Forms

The MBO approach originally focused on management or professional positions. It was designed to evaluate progress toward and completion of individual objectives designed to support overall

Figure 5-3   Job-Specific Performance Review Form

EMPLOYEE PERFORMANCE RATING

Employee Name: Last   First   Middle   Department:_____

Position _____   Employment Date:

Duties are specific job tasks that are performed on a day-to-day basis.
Responsibilities are collections of duties or behaviors that lead to an end result.
They reflect the results of performing several duties (*Note*: Attach updated position
description).

DUTIES AND/OR RESPONSIBILITIES:

	5 4 3 2 1
	5 4 3 2 1
	5 4 3 2 1
	5 4 3 2 1
	5 4 3 2 1
	5 4 3 2 1

Overall   5. Outstanding ____   3. Competent ____
Rating   4. Commendable ____   2. Acceptable ____   1. Unsatisfactory ____

Comments: (Include any pertinent points not covered above, such as outstanding traits
or areas for improvement. Use other side of page if necessary.)

_____

Employee Comments: (Use other side of page if necessary.)

Employee Signature _____   Date _____
                              (I have read this evaluation.)

Supervisor Signature _____   Date _____

company objectives. With a little imagination, the concept can be adapted to lower-level positions in a much smaller enterprise.

At the beginning of the performance review period, work with the individual employee in establishing specific work-related objectives. The best objectives are those that are measurable. For example, objectives for the switchboard operator and receptionist (with backup word processing duties) could be the following:

- Increase computer keyboarding skills from 30 wpm to 45 wpm during the review period. (Results will be measured by a typing test at the end of the review period.)
- Demonstrate proficiency in x number of functions (identify) of the Wordperfect 5.1 program by (specify date).
- Reduce customer complaints concerning receptionist by x number during the review period.
- Train two backup receptionists (identify by name) on main switchboard functions by (specify date).

Keep in mind that people are unique, bringing different skills, experience, and motivation to the job. Goals may differ for employees holding similar positions, reflecting their level of experience, ability, and maturity. Pick challenging yet achievable goals that can be measured accurately. To maintain credibility, success must be within the control of the employee. Never hold people accountable for results when they have little control over the processes required for success.

MBO requires frequent follow up, so keep a copy of the objectives close at hand. Interim progress reviews should be made, providing you have the opportunity to help the employee keep on track, lending support and providing adjustments when appropriate. Look for opportunities to reinforce good results and provide honest praise. Remember that with the rapid changes seen in many small businesses today, some objectives may become obsolete or alter in their value to the company.

The Upside
The beauty of MBO is its flexibility. Also, it focuses more on the job than on personality traits, as does job-specific evaluation.

The employee knows ahead of time what is to be accomplished during the review period.

The Downside

- Extra time and effort must be taken to establish clear, measurable objectives. Few workers have complete control over their work environment. Also, in order to obtain a good rating the employee may focus so much time on the objectives that normal day-to-day duties are neglected. This can usually be resolved with a combination approach. A sample MBO form is provided in Figure 5-4.

Combination Forms

Since no one technique covers everything, some owners have created evaluation forms combining both the traditional and MBO approach. See Figure 5-5 for an example.

PROGRAM ADMINISTRATION

The Frequency of Reviews

> *To everything there is a season,*
> *a time for every purpose under heaven . . .*
> *a time to keep silence, and a time to speak.*
> *—Ecclesiastes 3:1–7*

The frequency of reviews varies among organizations. One popular approach is to review newer employees after the first three or six months, after that annually. Many firms schedule their reviews on the employee's anniversary date, spreading the work over the course of the year. Others choose to do all reviews at the end of each calendar or fiscal year. A variety of approaches are taken by owners who schedule performance reviews with raises. Some may review employees every six months until their salary reaches a certain level, at which point reviews are performed annually.

Note: It is recommended that you still do performance reviews even though no raises follow. Even without a raise, performance expectations should be met.

Figure 5-4   MBO Performance Review Form

EMPLOYEE PERFORMANCE OBJECTIVES

Employee Name: Last   First   Middle   Department:_____

Position _____   Employment Date:

Objective 1:

_____ Target Date: _____

Results:_____ Met:___ Unmet:___

Objective 2:

_____ Target Date: _____

Results:_____ Met:___ Unmet:___

Objective 3:

_____ Target Date: _____

Results:_____ Met:___ Unmet:___

Objective 4:

_____ Target Date: _____

Results:_____ Met:___ Unmet:___

Objective 5:

_____ Target Date: _____

Results:_____ Met:___ Unmet:___

Employee Comments:

Supervisor Comments:

Employee's Signature:_____   Date:_____

Supervisor's Signature: _____   Date:_____

Figure 5-5 Combination Performance Review Form

EMPLOYEE PERFORMANCE RATING

| Employee Name: | Last | First | Middle | Department:_____ |

Position _____ Employment Date:

PERFORMANCE FACTORS
(Circle one in each category.)

Quality — **What is the quality of this employee's work?**
Does extremely high quality work 5
Work quality is usually above required standards 4
Meets required standards...3
Sometimes below standards 2
Unsatisfactory 1

Quantity — **Does the employee meet the quantity standards for the position?**
Exceptionally high producer 5
Quantity is usually above standards 4
Meets quantity standards...3
Sometimes below standards 2
Unsatisfactory 1

Teamwork — **Is the employee a team worker?**
Outstanding team worker 5
Works very well with others 4
Teamwork ability meets required level to perform the job 3
Is not always cooperative..2
Unsatisfactory 1

Dependability — **How dependable is this employee?**
Extremely reliable 5
Very reliable, requires little supervision 4
Reliable, requires average supervision.......................................3
Requires above-average supervision 2
Unsatisfactory 1

Objective: _____
_____ Target Date: _____

Results:_____ Met:___ Unmet:___

Objective: _____
_____ Target Date: _____

Results:_____ Met:___ Unmet:___

(continued)

Figure 5-5   *Continued*

Objective: _____

_____ Target Date: _____

_____

Results: _____ Met:___ Unmet:___

Objective: _____

_____ Target Date: _____

_____

Results: _____ Met:___ Unmet:___

Objective: _____

_____ Target Date: _____

_____

Results: _____ Met:___ Unmet:___

Objective: _____

_____ Target Date: _____

_____

Results: _____ Met:___ Unmet:___

Overall	5. Outstanding _____	3. Competent _____	
Rating	4. Commendable _____	2. Acceptable _____	1. Unsatisfactory _____

Comments: (Include any pertinent points not covered above, such as outstanding traits, or areas for improvement. Use other side of page if necessary.)

Employee Comments: (Use other side of page if necessary.)

Employee Signature _____ Date _____
                            (I have read this evaluation.)

Supervisor Signature _____ Date _____

Employee Participation

Actively involve employees in performance reviews. Obtaining their ideas and comments facilitates better cooperation. One method is to allow each employee to rate him- or herself on a separate review form prior to the formal review. You'll learn how employees see their own performance, perhaps confirming your evaluations. Employees may underrate their achievements, which gives you the opportunity to motivate them by raising their scores. Even if they overrate themselves you may gain a new perspective. Sometimes the employee will highlight achievements or problems you have overlooked. You can then focus on these areas.

Substantiating Reviews

Do you look at things according to outward appearance?
—II Corinthians 10:7

An entrepreneur conducting a performance review should be able to back up the assessment with as many facts as possible. Gut feelings and estimates don't cut it when challenged by an intelligent, assertive employee who wants to know why he or she received a certain rating. The fairest ratings are substantiated in a number of ways:

- *Work records.* Whenever possible keep good records of accomplished tasks. Granted, this may not be possible for many jobs, particularly administrative support and technical positions for which it may be difficult to quantify the work. Try to keep records that capture measures of quantity, quality, and turn around time. Including statistics on customer complaints should also be considered.
- *Observed behavior.* Take note of employee performance throughout the entire review period, not just the last few weeks before the evaluation. Employees know when they are due for a review; some play the system by stepping up their efforts a few weeks before the event or cultivating a more favorable impression in other ways.

An effective way to keep good performance notes is to create a page for each employee in your day planner. Under headings marked

Things Done Well and Areas for Improvement, note both good and bad performance incidents observed throughout the review period, including the date. Keep these notes confidential. Yes, you are literally keeping book on your employees, so don't go overboard and nit-pick; record only key incidents that will help you when it comes time to write the review. Praise your employees for good work and correct them quickly when bad performance occurs.

By keeping good notes you'll be amazed at how much backup material you have gathered. The time and effort spent will be more than offset by the speed and ease with which you will complete the review form later on.

Writing the Review

Referring to your observation notes and the employee's self-evaluation (if you allow it), clearly hand write the review in pencil. This allows you some flexibility when discussing your evaluation with the employee. You may find that you have overlooked something and decide to make changes. A typed review, signed in advance, signals to the employee that your comments are cast in bronze with no room for discussion.

The Performance Review Meeting

Every performance review meeting should be held privately and without interruption. Always start with the positive behaviors you have observed. Go over the rating with the employee step-by-step, allowing time to clarify issues and answer questions and concerns. Unless the review is simply outstanding, never present it over lunch.

Negative aspects can be presented as areas that need improvement. If performance is so bad you are considering termination, the review form can also serve as a warning. Under supervisory comments you can note that the employee has been placed in warning status due to poor performance. When the employee signs the acknowledgment line he or she confirms awareness of the warning as well.

During the review meeting don't forget to discuss the employee's future expectations, career goals, training needs, and development issues. If using the MBO approach, work with your employees in setting objectives for the next review period.

> *And do as adversaries do in law,*
> *strike mightily, but eat and drink as friends.*
> —*William Shakespeare*

In recent years many firms have discontinued awarding raises at the same time the performance review is given. Experience has shown that combining the two can obscure effective discussion of employee performance. Performance is discussed at one meeting, and a second session is scheduled for some months later to talk about money.

Multirater Assessments

> *Never judge till you've heard the other side.*
> —*Euripides*

Larger corporations have been incorporating multirater programs, and there really isn't any reason you as an entrepreneur cannot experiment as well. In a multirater system, input on employee performance is not limited to just the employee's boss. Feedback is solicited from fellow employees within a work team, internal customers, outside customers, and even subordinates if the person being rated supervises people. When the system is adequately controlled, good results are reported.

The employee knows in advance that the review is not just from the boss, but rather will incorporate input from others inside and perhaps outside the company.

Essential Documentation

Written performance reviews can be essential documentation justifying employer actions in a court of law. Contested terminations, failure to promote, downgrades, job reassignments, and contested training opportunities are some examples of when the information in a performance review can be invaluable. In layoff situations, accurate performance reviews can help determine who gets terminated and who doesn't.

Designing Your Performance Review Form

With modern word processing equipment you may consider designing your own form to suit your business and personal preference. A list of performance factors common to industry is included in Figure 5-6.

Figure 5-6   Performance Factors

Knowledge
Job Knowledge
Professional and Technical Knowledge
Administrative Know-How
Computer System Knowledge

Skills
Problem-Solving Skills
Administrative Skills
Communication Skills
Interpersonal Skills

Abilities
Gets the Job Done
Manages the Job
Judgment/Decision Making
Reasoning
Ability to Handle Stress

Quality
Quality of Work
Concern for Quality
Accuracy

Quanity
Work Production
Quantity of Work

Teamwork/Work Relations
Teamwork
Cooperation
Interaction with Others
Work Relationships

Appearance
Personal Appearance
Neatness
Dress and Grooming

Personal Characteristics
Dependability
Versatility
Adaptability
Flexibility
Cooperativeness
Effectiveness
Assertiveness
Alertness
Promptness
Motivation
Drive
Initiative
Reasonable Risk-Taking Ability
Enthusiasm
Work Habits

Customer Service
Customer Responsiveness
Customer Service
Client Relations
Acceptance by Customers
Friendliness
Courtesy

Creativity
Creativity
Ideas
Original Thinking
Resourcefulness

Cost Control
Budgetary Controls
Economy
Expense Management

Management and Supervisory Skills
Supervisory Skills
Managing Employees
Coaching/Counseling
Responsibility and Planning
Staff Training and Development
Development of Subordinates
Professional Development
Delegation Skills
Leadership
Time Management
Planning and Goal Setting
Professional Conduct

Other
Safety and Health
Attendance and Punctuality

Guidelines for Entrepreneurs and Small Business Owners

Performance Evaluation

Doing employee performance reviews is a real hassle for many owners. Many of the smallest firms avoid them altogether. After all, there is no law that says that you must do them. Once a year the employee may get a raise and a few words such as "Keep up the good work." Even this is something.

Problems can arise, however, when poor performers are *not* told their work is substandard. It doesn't really make much sense to let an employee go on doing a poor job without some sort of feedback. As the owner you can choose to take just about any approach to performance reviews. Keep in mind the following:

- With only a few jobs to manage consider using the job-specific form outlined in Figure 5-3.
- List on the form the key duties and responsibilities most important for the job, but don't forget to get input from the workers actually performing these tasks.
- Performance feedback should never be a once-a-year event. Your employees should get frequent input from you, including praise and discussion of areas in need of improvement.
- With performance feedback given in a courteous and frequent manner, the results of the annual review should be no surprise to the employee.

6

CORRECTIVE ACTION

Hopefully, you're an entrepreneur blessed with a terrific staff anxious to come to work each day and give their best. Still, you're dealing with people. Sooner or later you'll encounter employee behavior problems requiring corrective action on your part in order to protect your business. In its mildest form, corrective action may comprise just a few words of advice. That may be all that is needed to resolve the matter. More serious problems may require multiple meetings with the employee, followed by written warnings. Some problems may require exercising corporate capital punishment: involuntary termination.

The larger the staff, the greater the potential for problems. Society has problems, people make up society, and most people work. Every business gets its share of difficult people. Careful recruiting, good wages, and fair employment practices can go a long way toward keeping problems to a minimum, yet nothing is absolute.

As the owner, you can institute policies and programs that minimize employee problems and enable employees to better balance work and life issues.

POLICIES SUPPORTING GOOD ATTENDANCE

Poor attendance is a universal problem. It includes excessive absence and/or lateness. What is excessive depends on the job and the owner's expectations. Unlike other employee problems it's the easiest behavior to observe: the employee is either in or out. Employers have had some success in resolving this problem by meeting employees half way with flexible approaches to workplace schedules.

Staggered Work Hours

Provided your production and/or customer service needs are being met, you may be able to allow some workers to start and leave earlier in the day. A 7:00 A.M. to 3:00 P.M. work schedule can be quite popular with some working parents. It enables them to be home for their children when school lets out. Other employees may prefer to work a 10:00 A.M. to 6:00 P.M. schedule. In congested urban areas, heavy early morning traffic can be avoided this way. Under this staggered arrangement, employees are given a choice of schedules. Once chosen, they must stick with it consistently and have any changes approved in advance by management.

Flextime

Under a flextime system, employees must be present during specific core hours, for example, from 10:00 A.M. to 3:00 P.M. Beyond these core hours they have flexibility on arrivals and departures each day so long as they put in the required 7- to 8-hour workday and meet production or service standards. Additional administrative effort may be required for keeping track of employee hours. Companies using time clocks should have less of a problem. For the entrepreneur, a successful flextime program should reduce the role of time cop for monitoring employee lateness.

Compressed Workweek

By extending daily working hours, employees work a four-day rather than five-day workweek followed by a three-day weekend with either Mondays or Fridays off.

Work-at-Home Programs

With modern telecommunications tools such as pagers, cellular phones, answering machines, modems, and faxes, work-at-home programs will become more practical. Think of the gas and commuting expense saved, plus lower clothing and dry-cleaning costs. If quality, quantity, and customer service standards are maintained, does it really matter where some work is performed? Depending on your business, perhaps not.

Time Made Up

Employees can be allowed to make up lost time before or after normal working hours. Again, feasibility depends on the nature of the work, the business, and how much supervision is required. Security is another concern. You may not wish to have employees making up for lost time alone at night or on weekends. Also, the work may require support systems, such as computer programs, not available after normal working hours.

For better control, decisions to allow time to be made up should be made by the owner. Making up time is a privilege usually not granted to low performers with chronic attendance problems.

Note: For nonexempt hourly workers, time made up should be completed within the same workweek within which the time off was taken to avoid possible overtime obligations under the Fair Labor Standards Act (FLSA). For example, if the company's normal work week is 40 hours and an employee misses five hours one week, but is permitted to make up the time the *following* week by working 45 hours, the owner could be held liable for overtime pay for the 45-hour week.

No-Fault Absences

For many employees, paid sick leave is considered a privilege of employment. They feel the owner owes them these days, sick or not. They abuse the program and call in sick for minor ailments or other reasons not involving illness. They feel entitled to this time.

Under traditional paid sick leave programs, owners are routinely placed in the position of assessing the credibility of employee excuses, which places stress on both parties. Some employers have merged vacation and sick leave programs into one. The employee can use these days for vacation, personal appointments, or illness under a no-fault arrangement. No excuse is required. When the allotment is exhausted, no additional paid days are provided.

Attendance Incentive Programs

Recognizing and rewarding good attendance behavior with an incentive award can be very effective. Consider the following:

- *Pay for unused sick leave.* Consider paying for a portion of accrued but unused sick leave at the end of each calendar year.
- *Additional time off for good attendance.* Employees with good annual attendance records are given extra paid vacation or personal days as a reward.
- *Gift certificates.* For employees with good attendance.
- *Reserved parking spot.* Allow the employee to use a reserved parking space for a full month. This is great benefit in areas where parking spaces are at a premium.

Management by Example

Often overlooked is the importance of setting a good example for employees. If your supervisor has poor attendance habits, how can you expect cooperation from the workers? The privileges of rank don't hold much value in their eyes if the people in charge are persistently late or absent.

PERFORMANCE PROBLEMS

The reasons for poor performance are not always obvious. Before taking punitive action consider the following:

- Does the employee try, but in fact lack the work skills to perform up to standards? Perhaps retraining would help.
- Does the employee know the standards of performance for the job? Do you have any standards? Most people want to do a good job but may have no idea what is expected of them.
- Can the job be adjusted to better match the employee's ability? You don't have to lower your standards but perhaps some parts of the job can be assigned to someone else.
- Is the employee underutilized, performing duties far below capabilities? Can you provide more challenging assignments?
- Can you do some job rotation, even temporarily?

Personal Problems

Employee personal problems do spill over into the workplace. They can sap the morale of others, hurting production and customer service. The employee may be going through a temporary domestic, financial, or health problem. If you're supportive, good workers remember that you stood by them in a crisis.

For some employees the problem is not temporary; their whole life may seem a mess. Alcohol and drug abuse may be present. Few entrepreneurs are qualified to counsel people with such problems. Professional help may be needed and if the employee doesn't seek it, he or she may eventually be fired. This is one reason for the rapid growth of employee assistance programs (EAPs).

Many employers, particularly the larger ones, contract with EAP providers to counsel employees with problems. The early programs focused primarily on drug and alcohol abuse but now include counseling for marital and family problems, spousal abuse, excessive gambling and spending habits, and other disorders. Credentialed professionals counsel employees in confidence and/or refer them to other appropriate services. Proven cost effective, they have helped employees resolve and recover from personal crisis. The employer benefits with improved productivity, reduced turnover, and reduced health insurance claim costs.

EAPs coordinate their services with health insurance programs sponsored by employers. The number of visits allowed may be limited by the policy restrictions on psychological disorders. EAPs can be an important tool within the corrective action process. These programs enable owners to refer the employee to an outside source for help while avoiding involvement in personal matters best handled by professionals. However, employees must seek help voluntarily.

THE CORRECTIVE ACTION PROCESS

Sound personnel policies are effective in preventing problems from getting out of hand or developing in the first place. Nonetheless, direct intervention by the employer is often needed to resolve persistent problems of a serious nature. Traditionally called disciplinary action or progressive discipline, the term corrective action is popular today. It sounds less punitive, but involves basically the same process, which includes (1) one or two oral discussions or warnings, (2) a first written warning, and (3) a final written warning.

The Oral Warning

To administer an oral warning, meet privately with the employee, explaining the issue as you see it and how it is affecting operations. Try to focus on the problem behavior rather than personal characteristics. Give the employee an opportunity to explain, listening carefully. Seek a verbal commitment to correct the problem and offer your support. Take notes summarizing the meeting including the date, time, key issues, and commitments made.

If the problem continues, hold a second meeting. Go over the problem again, insisting on improvement and still offering your support. Remind the employee of his or her commitment to resolve the situation. Again, keep good notes.

Give the employee a reasonable period of time to correct the problem. What is reasonable will depend on the nature of the problem; but don't go beyond a week or two without taking further action. If no improvements are forthcoming, a second oral warning is in order.

If after two verbal warnings there is no improvement, a third meeting is held. However, this time advise the employee that he or she will be receiving a written warning summarizing the problem. Sample of first warning memos are provided in Figures 6-1 and 6-2.

Note: The employee may respond with his or her own memo. Accept it, keeping it in the individual's personnel file, but avoid getting into memo wars. You've made your case, so stick to your course of action unless new facts pertinent to the situation compel you to change direction.

Although no one likes being written up, warnings are useful in clarifying the issues involved in poor performance. Putting the situation in writing provides more impact. Good documentation is essential in case termination results and a lawsuit follows. It can demonstrate that you follow a graduated, formal process to resolve employee problems. Assume that anything you put in writing may ultimately be read by an outside attorney, administrative hearing officer, judge, or jury. If the employee achieves the desired improvement, congratulations! Think of all the recruiting effort and training time you've saved by not having to hire a replacement. If improvement is not achieved you may choose to provide another oral warning or move on to the final written warning. Samples are provided in Figures 6-3 and 6-4.

TERMINATION

Because of the corrective action process, an actual firing may be no surprise to the employee. Once you have made the decision, plan the event carefully. Your purpose is to exit the individual as

Figure 6-1   First Written Warning Due to Poor Attendance

Memo to: _____

From: _____

Date: _____

Subject: Warning due to poor attendance

This memo is to confirm our meeting on _____
regarding your poor attendance. We discussed this problem on
_____ and again on _____, when you were advised of
the need to improve work attendance. So far this year, our time sheet
records indicate that you have been absent on the following days, most of
them reflecting a pattern of Monday or Friday absences:

_____   _____
_____   _____
_____   _____
_____   _____
_____   _____

Your absenteeism continues to have a serious impact on operation, causing
delays in timely processing and impairing our ability to promptly serve
our customers. It is also causing hardship for your coworkers who must
perform your duties in addition to their own when you are absent.

Immediate and sustained improvement in your attendance is required and
will be closely monitored over the next 20 working days. If improvement is
not forthcoming during this period, additional corrective action will be
taken, up to and including the possibility of termination of employment.

_____
A. J. Jones, Owner

cc: Personnel File   _____
                                                 (Acknowledged)

Figure 6-2   First Written Warning Due to Unsatisfactory Performance

Memo to: _____

From: _____

Date: _____

Subject: Warning due to unsatisfactory performance

This memo is to confirm our meeting on _____ regarding unsatisfactory work performance. I had discussed this with you on _____ and again on _____, when you were advised of the need to produce at least 50 units per day. This is the minimum number of units required in order for us to meet our daily shipping schedule.

It is expected that the time we spent reviewing work procedures will assist you in meeting this standard. Also, a reduction in unnecessary socializing with coworkers should enable you to better focus your work efforts.

I will continue to be available to help you with any questions or problems you may have. Your progress will be closely monitored during the next 10 working days with a follow-up meeting scheduled for _____ to assess progress.

_____

A. J. Jones, Owner

_____

cc: Personnel File   (Acknowledged)

Figure 6-3   Final Written Warning Due to Poor Attendance

Memo to: _____

From: _____

Date: _____

Subject: Final warning due to poor attendance

This memo serves as notification that effective today you are on "final warning" for poor work attendance.

Since your written warning of _____ you have been absent the following days without appropriate substantiation:

_____

_____

You are again reminded that immediate and sustained improvement is essential. Your poor attendance behavior is continuing to have a negative effect on your fellow employees who must complete your work when you are out, company production, and service to our customers.

Any further absences without good cause will result in your <u>termination of employment.</u>

_____
A. J. Jones, Owner

cc: Personnel File   _____
                                                          (Acknowledged)

Figure 6-4   Final Written Warning Due to Unsatisfactory Performance

Memo to: _____

From: _____

Date: _____

Subject: Final warning due to unsatisfactory performance

This memo is to confirm our meeting yesterday regarding unsatisfactory work performance. Unfortunately, during your 10-day monitoring period the minimum required production of 50 units per day was not achieved. As a result, we were unable to meet daily shipping schedules on a timely basis.

You are again reminded that immediate and sustained improvement in your work performance is essential. If these work standards are not achieved quickly, termination of your employment will result.

_____

A. J. Jones, Owner

_____

cc: Personnel File   (Acknowledged) smoothly and quietly as possible. Complete all administrative details such as the following in advance:

- Termination letter
- Arrangements for the final paycheck
- Security arrangements
- Disposition of personal property
- Timing the termination

The Termination Letter

The termination letter should be prepared on company letterhead, indicate the effective date, and outline the reasons for dismissal including particulars for any severance pay arrangements. See Figures 6-5 and 6-6 for samples.

The Final Paycheck

If the termination is between paydays, you'll have time for an adjusted check to be prepared and mailed to the person's home address or processed through direct deposit. Nonetheless, you may want to have this check ready at termination. Don't forget to clear any outstanding cash advances.

Security Arrangements

Arrangements should be made to prevent those dismissed from reentering your facilities and systems. A good checklist will remind you to collect company ID cards, office and desk keys, keys to company vehicles, card access keys, and so forth. Be sure to alert the security force, if any, that the person is no longer allowed access.

If for any reason you fear a violent reaction from the terminated employee, you may wish to have a security person or another member of management alerted and close by during the termination meeting, ready to come to your support if necessary.

Figure 6-5   Termination-of-Employment Letter Due to Poor Attendance

---

On Company Letterhead

Date:

_____

_____

_____

Dear_____:

This letter is to confirm your termination of employment with
_____, Inc., effective _____ for excessive
absenteeism.

As you are aware, your poor attendance and the need for immediate
improvement was discussed with you personally in my office on the following dates:

_____   _____

_____   _____

A written warning addressing this problem was given to you on
_____. Because no improvement was forthcoming, a *final* written
warning was issued on _____. Since that date your pattern of
absences has continued, causing delays in production and customer service. This pattern of behavior can no longer be tolerated, resulting in this
necessary decision to terminate your employment.

Information regarding your rights to continue health benefits at your
expense will be mailed to you shortly by certified letter.

We wish you success in your future career pursuits.

Sincerely,

A. J. Jones, Owner

cc: Personnel File

Figure 6-6   Termination-of-Employment Letter Due to
Unsatisfactory Performance

On Company Letterhead

_____   Date: _____
_____
_____

Dear_____:

This letter will confirm your termination of employment with
_____, Inc., effective _____ for unsatisfactory
work performance.

As you are aware, your unsatisfactory performance and the need for immediate improvement was discussed with you personally in my office on the
following dates:

_____   _____

_____   _____

A written warning addressing this problem was given to you on _____.
Because no improvement was forthcoming, a *final* written warning was
issued to you on _____. Since that date your pattern of unsatisfactory performance has continued, causing delays in production and poor
customer service. This pattern of behavior can no longer be tolerated,
resulting in the necessary decision to terminate your employment.

Information regarding your rights to continue health benefits at your
expense will be mailed to you shortly by certified letter.

We wish you success in your future career pursuits.

Sincerely,

A. J. Jones, Owner

cc: Personnel File

Disposition of Personal Property

Assistance should be provided to enable the terminated employee to pack up any personal belongings and carry them from the premises. Items left behind can be mailed later so be sure you have the employee's latest home address.

Timing the Termination

The termination meeting should be held at a time and place that will afford the employee as much privacy as possible. Early in the morning before others arrive for work is one approach. Waiting until closing time only prolongs the tension, and there is always the possibility that the employee will find out ahead of schedule. Just before a weekend is not recommended. If let go during the work-week, a person can start a job search that much sooner and won't stew over a weekend.

The Termination Meeting

During the termination meeting be professional but firm and to the point. Explain the reason for termination as clearly and briefly as possible. Ensure the reason coincides with any prior written warnings and the termination letter.

If you have done a thorough job during the corrective action process, being fired may not be a shock to the employee. Some may wonder what took you so long and be relieved that it is finally over. Never assume this reaction, however. Some people, no matter how many times you warn them, never really think they will be fired. They may discount even a final warning memo. People who are fired may react with shock, tears, or anger so allow time for them to compose themselves. Avoid argument, long discussions, or post-mortems.

Give the employee the original of the termination letter. If the employee is eligible for COBRA health insurance continuation, advise that a certified letter will outline his or her rights.

Request office keys, company ID card, or other company property. If you have it prepared, give the employee the final paycheck; if not, confirm his or her home address so the check can be mailed. When finished, stand up and wish the person well, ending the session. If you escort your former employee out of the building, do so as unobtrusively as possible.

References

The former employee, now faced with finding a new job, may ask what sort of references you'll provide. If your policy is to provide neutral references (i.e., dates of employment, position, or confirmation of salary), say so. If your policy is to provide more detailed information regarding reasons for termination (performance, attendance record, etc.), consult with your attorney before responding to reference requests, particularly for someone you fired.

Terminations for Cause

Most terminations are for one cause or another, but the phrase termination for cause has come to indicate quick firings caused by more serious circumstances. Occasionally, employers will terminate someone for gross misconduct, which is behavior so serious that the step-by-step corrective action process would be impractical. Examples of what is termed gross misconduct include the following:

- Theft or deliberate damage of company property
- Possession, sale, or distribution of illegal drugs
- Being under the influence of alcohol or drugs
- Fighting
- Fraud
- Falsifying company records, including false recording of time worked
- Unauthorized disclosure of confidential or proprietary information

When gross misconduct is discovered, emotions can run very high. You may need time to make a thorough investigation of all the facts before taking action and consult with your attorney.

Under some circumstances, such as fighting or drunkenness, sending the employee home for the day may defuse the issue and allow time to arrive at a clear decision.

Unemployment Benefits Eligibility

Terminated employees will go to the local state unemployment office to apply for benefits. The unemployment office will mail your company a questionnaire requesting confirmation of the person's employment dates, salary, and the particulars regarding the termination. They use this information to determine whether or not to pay benefits and may call you to ask additional questions regarding the termination, making a decision based on input received from both you and the terminated employee.

If unemployment benefits are awarded to the employee, costs will be charged against the company's unemployment experience record. This can affect the unemployment insurance rates you pay.

There is a process of appeals for unemployment decisions. At a scheduled hearing at the unemployment office both sides can state their case and provide testimony, documentation, and witnesses. The unemployment office may approve benefits for someone fired due to poor performance if they surmise that the individual tried to perform but did not have the ability. An example would be if the company hired or transferred someone into a position for which the person was very obviously not qualified. In this case, the company may have to assume the responsibility for making a poor decision. Benefits can also be extended to someone fired for poor attendance if it appears that management was lax or unclear in communicating expectations.

If your documentation is incomplete, you may decide not to challenge unemployment compensation payments. A terminated employee may be less likely to file discrimination charges if the loss is tempered by a weekly unemployment check.

Publicity

Be careful what is communicated to existing employees regarding terminated employees. Most will surmise that a person was fired and the reasons for that action. You are under no obligation to confirm it. Termination is normally a private, confidential matter. Those who worked with the individual can be told that he or she is no longer in your employ. End of story. Some entrepreneurs, with the intent of setting an example for other workers, have provided the details of firings to their employees and ended up defending a defamation (slandering the good name or reputation of another) lawsuit by the terminated employee.

Exercise the same caution with inquiries from outside the company (e.g., friends, customers, and vendors). Your receptionist or switchboard person should simply advise inquiring outsiders that the individual is no longer with the company.

Guidelines for Entrepreneurs
and Small Business Owners

Corrective Action

You have the advantage over larger corporations when it comes to the corrective action process. You can move quickly and with much more flexibility. With only a few people to supervise you can better experiment with some of the alternatives listed in this chapter for addressing attendance and performance problems, keeping those that work best for you.

It is inevitable that you'll have to apply discipline to help some people focus on performing or getting to work on time. If you do demote, suspend, or fire someone and are later sued, your best defense is good documentation. It's often true that he who documents best wins! Attorneys, courts, juries, unemployment hearing officers, and the Equal Employment Opportunity Commission all look for good documentation when processing cases. The key things they look for include the following:

- Does the owner have a corrective action process in place?
- Is it being followed fairly and consistently with all employees?
- Does it allow the employee enough time to correct the problem?

As a busy owner you may not have the time or patience to go through all the oral and written warnings mentioned in this chapter. But remember, it is important that you keep good documentation on whatever actions you do take and be ready to prove that corrective action has been applied fairly and consistently in your attempts to resolve the problem.

7

EMPLOYEE BENEFITS

Company-sponsored insurance benefits have become an important part of the employee's total compensation package. The recent controversy over national health insurance illustrates how important health benefits are to the employer-employee relationship.

The growth of employee benefits since World War II has been substantial. Unions were the main force throughout these years, bargaining with employers for expanded benefit packages for their members. In order to compete for workers, nonunion firms followed suit with their own benefits programs. The Bureau of Labor Statistics (BLS) reports that employee benefits currently average 28.4 percent of total compensation in private industry. The government is now a most powerful force in both regulating existing programs and mandating new ones.

Entrepreneurs often use an insurance broker to solicit proposals from local insurance companies. Brokers analyze the different proposals and recommend a vendor. Acting as middlemen, many add their expertise and save time for the owner. Remember though, brokers are paid a commission by the vendor they select. The cost of this commission is passed on to you in higher premium rates. Brokers may not always act in your best interest if they enjoy sweetheart pacts with specific vendors that offer better commissions. As a result, you may not always get the best product at the best price.

Unless you decide to perform your own vendor solicitation and analysis, you might consider calling your local state insurance department office and ask them to provide a list of certified insurance consultants. They might even recommend a few. By paying a consultant his or her fee directly, you may get a more objective analysis and a better product for a lower premium.

Covered in the first part of this chapter are benefits that organizations provide to their employees through insurance programs. The overview is divided into two sections: mandated benefits and those provided voluntarily at the discretion of the employer. Covered in the second half of this chapter are time off benefits such as vacation, sick days, and so forth.

MANDATED BENEFITS

As the term implies, you have no choice but to provide mandated benefits to your employees. They are required by law and their costs are substantial. Don't lose sight of these costs when managing your payroll budget. The Bureau of Labor Statistics reports that mandated benefits now average 8.7 percent of total compensation. Mandated benefits include social security, unemployment insurance, and workers' compensation programs.

Social Security

Social security comprises the old age retirement, survivor, disability, and medicare health insurance programs (OASDHI). All employees are taxed via employee payroll deduction which is currently 7.65 percent of individual gross wages up to an annual limit. This limit is adjusted periodically to adjust for inflation. The 7.65 percent employee deduction must be matched by you, the employer. These are your FICA (Federal Insurance Contributions Act) taxes which must be deposited on a timely basis.

Unemployment Insurance

Designed to provide wages to unemployed workers, unemployment insurance is mandated by the Federal Unemployment Tax Act (FUTA) and administered by individual states, so benefits and employee eligibility requirements vary (26 weeks of benefits is most common).

The cost of unemployment insurance is paid for primarily by the business owner and the premiums are collected via federal and state unemployment payroll taxes as a percentage of payroll. The tax rate is based on a company's unemployment history or experience.

Note: A few states require employee contributions to unemployment insurance in addition to the contribution made by the owner. These mandated contributions are also collected through payroll withholding taxes. If you have employees located in these states you can find out the required employee withholding percentage by contacting your accountant, your outside payroll service if you have one, or that state's unemployment office. These states are Alabama, Alaska, New Jersey, and Pennsylvania.

Workers' Compensation

Workers' compensation programs are administered by the states and are designed to cover employees incurring job-related injury, death, or illness. Workers' compensation programs include the following benefits:

- Hospital, surgical, and medical costs for work-related injuries or diseases
- Rehabilitation services
- Cash payments for lost wages
- Death benefits for dependent survivors, including income support and funeral and burial expenses for the deceased employee
- Partial or total disability benefits for temporary or permanent disabilities

The premiums (insurance coverage fees) are paid by the business owner. The rates are based on industry classification groups, some of which incur higher risk than others (e.g., the construction trades and heavy manufacturing). Workers' compensation insurance rates are charged as a certain number of dollars for each $100 of payroll. Because employee risks for work-related injury or disease differ by job classification, insurance rates vary widely.

For smaller employers, workers' compensation insurance is purchased through insurance companies. Insurance auditors will come on site to review your payroll and examine the different kinds of workers employed to confirm they are being classified correctly. The larger firms self-insure these benefits, a concept covered elsewhere in this chapter.

Some states require the employer to purchase workers' compensation insurance for its employees through a state agency. These states are Nevada, North Dakota, Ohio, Washington, West Virginia, and Wyoming.

Workers' compensation costs, particularly for health care, have been rising dramatically each year, capturing national attention. Some of the more progressive states have installed modern cost control programs, such as managed health care, which require more intensive oversight of physicians' fees and better administrative controls. For employers, workplace safety programs are essential to help reduce exposure to expensive injury claims.

VOLUNTARY BENEFITS

The provision of voluntary benefits is up to the employer. So far, the government doesn't require that you provide them. Many small firms can't afford benefits beyond those legally required or mandated. Others must provide additional voluntary benefits to attract and retain good employees. Voluntary benefits covered in this chapter include the following:

- Hospitalization and medical/surgical plans
- Major medical and comprehensive health plans
- Prescription drug plans
- Dental plans

Figure 7-1   Annual Deductibles

The employee incurs a doctor's charge of $500. The annual deductible under the group plan stipulates $150 out-of-pocket expense before the insurance plan kicks in.

Employee first pays:	$150
Insurance plan then pays	$350
Total:	$500

- Vision care
- Managed care programs
- Short- and long-term disability plans
- Accidental death and dismemberment insurance
- Group life insurance
- Cafeteria programs

Insurance Terminology

Before going further let's go over some basic insurance terminology. You may want to read this standing up so it doesn't put you to sleep; it's pretty dry stuff!

- *Annual deductibles*—are the amount the employee must pay out of pocket before the group health insurance pays any costs or reimbursement. Each new year the annual deductible must be met before benefits are received. Deductibles are for both the individual employee and the

Figure 7-2   Coinsurance

The employee incurs a hospital expense of $5,000. The insurance plan specifies an 80%/20% coinsurance arrangement.

Employee pays:	20% × $5,000 = $1,000
Insurance plan pays:	80% × $5,000 = $4,000
Total:	$5,000

Figure 7-3   Deductible and Coinsurance Combined

Using the above doctor's fee of $500, a combination deductible and co-insurance would result in the following:

Employee pays deductible:	$150
Employee pays 20% of the remaining $350:	$70
Insurance plan pays 80% of the remaining $350:	$280
Total:	$500

family if the employee's dependents are enrolled under the plan. See Figure 7-1 for an example of how a typical deductible is calculated.

- *Coinsurance*—means the insurance plan will pay only a specified percentage of claim costs once benefit payments commence, usually after the deductible is met. The employee must pay the difference out of pocket. Figure 7-2 shows an example. In many plans both deductibles and coinsurance will apply, as described in Figure 7-3.

    It should be obvious that deductibles and coinsurance are cost reduction measures. The higher the deductible and copayment amounts for the employee, the less expensive the group insurance plan is to the business owner. Also, by requiring employees to foot some of the bills, it is hoped that overutilization of benefits can be minimized.

- *Premium sharing*—means that the employee shares a percentage of the cost of group heath insurance with the employer. See Figure 7-4 for an example. The number of employers paying the full premium cost for group health insurance on behalf of their employees has fallen dramatically in recent

Figure 7-4   Premium Sharing

If employee health insurance premium costs $200 per month,

Employee pays 20% of monthly costs via payroll withholding:	20% × $200 =	$40
Employer pays 80% of monthly costs:	80% × $200 =	$160
Total:		$200

years. How much will you require your employees to pay? Will it be 10 percent, 20 percent, or 25 percent? Premium sharing, along with deductible and copayment percentages are important variables to consider when planning your own benefits program.

Note: Under Section 125 of IRS regulations, employee-paid portions of group health insurance premiums can be deducted on a pretax basis from gross salary, exposing less of an employee's gross wages to taxes. Section 125 also allows companies to sponsor flexible spending accounts (covered later in this chapter).

- *Fee for service*—pertains to medical insurance plans in which physicians are paid a specified fee for specific services provided to the patient. A schedule of fees is published by the insurer covering these services.
- *Dependent Coverage*—is employer-sponsored insurance coverage for an employee's dependents. Many larger firms pay a percentage of dependent premium costs, for example, 40 to 50 percent or even more.

Health Benefits

Hospitalization Insurance Plans

Basic hospitalization plans cover room charges, general nursing services, operating and recovery rooms, intensive care units, diagnostic X-ray and lab exams, in-hospital drugs and medicines, use of blood transfusion equipment, testing equipment, anesthesia, dressings, biologicals, vaccines, and other medical supplies and services customarily provided by a hospital. Included is outpatient care, outpatient surgery, and use of emergency rooms. Most hospitalization insurance plans place limits on long-term illnesses or disabilities involving mental disorders, treatment for alcoholism, treatment for drug abuse, and admissions to the hospital for diagnostics tests with no subsequent treatment.

Basic Medical/Surgical Plans

Medical/surgical plans cover expenses such as physician diagnostic services, surgical fees, doctor's visits, certain types of therapy, and maternity care.

Major Medical Plans

Traditional major medical plans were designed to supplement basic hospitalization and medical benefits. After the insured absorbs a specified out-of-pocket deductible, major medical benefits cover additional charges above the basic programs (typically at 80 percent coverage), up to a maximum limit, for example, a million dollars.

Comprehensive Plans

Comprehensive plans combine features of both basic and major medical plans into a single package. An up-front deductible must usually be paid by the employee before coverage takes effect. After that deductible is met, the plan's benefits are effective and hospital/surgical/ medical charges are paid at a 70 or 80 percent rate. Depending on the plan, a lifetime benefits maximum may or may not apply.

Prescription Drug Plans

Prescription drug programs may be included as a part of a comprehensive or major medical health insurance plan. They can also be provided on a stand-alone basis and may include an annual deductible such that the plan pays 75 to 80 percent of prescription charges once this deductible is met. The drugs covered are limited to those legally requiring a prescription written by a licensed physician or dentist.

Dental Plans

Dental plans can be designed to include four categories of care with varying levels of coverage.

- *Basic care*—includes preventive and diagnostic services such as oral examinations, cleaning, X rays, fillings, simple extractions, and repair of dentures. In order to encourage employees to take care of their teeth before major problems occur, firms often choose to pay up to 100 percent of these expenses after an annual deductible is met. Many will pay on a graduated time scale: 70 or 80 percent in the first year, 80 to 90 percent for the second year, and 90 to 100 percent for the third year, provided the employee goes to the dentist every year, ultimately reducing claim costs.

- *Supplemental basic care*—can include surgical extractions, the excision of impacted teeth, treatment of fractures, treatment of cysts, surgical root canal therapy, crowns, inlays, and space maintainers. Coverage of 80 percent of expenses is an option.
- *Prosthetic care*—includes the installation or repair of fixed or removable bridges and the installation or replacement of dentures. Fifty percent coverage is a common amount.
- *Periodontal care*—includes exams, scale removal, and gum and bone surgery. After meeting a deductible, 50 percent coverage is standard.
- *Orthodontics*—is normally restricted to dependent children. Because of its expense, orthodontics coverage may not be an option you wish to include in your group dental plan. When included, coverage is frequently restricted to 50 percent of charges.

Vision Care

Vision care programs have grown in popularity mostly with larger organizations. Coverage includes items not normally covered in basic and major medical health programs, such as routine eye exams, eyeglasses, contact lenses, and the purchase and fitting of frames. Similar to other insured programs, deductible and coinsurance options apply.

Managed Care Provider Programs

Until recently, health care costs were rising at double-digit annual rates. Larger corporations with more negotiating leverage and buying power have been instrumental in slowing these costs with the managed care approach. Managed care is the health care delivery system proving (so far) to be the most effective in slowing the increase in health care costs. Most insurance companies offer managed care options, usually at lower premium rates. Managed care programs contain better cost control features than regular programs. Under the managed care umbrella are the following:

- *Health Maintenance Organizations (HMOs).* Health insurers contract with local HMOs, or set up their own HMO to service client companies and their employees. HMOs may operate on a prepaid basis for a given population. Operating from a central location or multiple locations, they provide one-stop shopping for a variety of health services. Stressing preventive care, the primary care physicians working in HMOs are salaried employees without the high overhead costs of a private practice. One way they manage care is by serving as gatekeepers when directing services, particularly by referring patients to an approved list of specialists outside of the HMO.

- *Preferred Provider Organizations (PPOs).* PPOs are networks of hospitals and physicians who provide discounted health care to corporations and their employees. Smaller businesses can purchase PPO-based services through insurance companies that also contract with PPOs.

The growth of managed care has not been without its difficulties. Some employees may be reluctant to opt for HMO or PPO networks because it may mean giving up their private physician. To address this problem many insurers include point of service arrangements in their group health plans.

Point of Service (POS)

POS plans give your employees the option of going to a participating physician within the HMO or PPO network, or outside the established network to another doctor. If they go outside the established HMO or PPO network, the employee must absorb additional out-of-pocket costs such as deductibles and/or copayments.

Self-Funding

Self-funding of employer health benefits has become increasingly popular. The large firms started the trend, but over the past few years the concept has spread to smaller businesses with as few as fifty employees.

Self-funding is self-insurance in which the employer pays employee health claims out of current revenues or from a separate trust fund financed by the employer. Companies that self-fund will hire an outside service (a third-party administrator) to administer the program, pay claims from the employer's health insurance fund, and handle employee claim problems.

The trend toward self-funding was caused by the rapid rise in the cost of health insurance premiums charged by insurance companies. A portion of these insurance company premiums comprise state premium taxes, insurance company overhead costs, reserves for unanticipated claims, and profit for the insurer. Self-funding eliminates most of these expenses. With most self-funded plans, the employer purchases medical stop loss insurance from a commercial insurance carrier that covers larger, more serious claims over an amount specified in advance. The stop loss carrier assumes this extra risk while the company focuses on paying the more frequently occurring lower-cost health claims.

Caution: Only healthy, profitable companies with good cash flow and the ability to handle the heavy administrative and legal work involved should consider self-funding. They should also have a good claims history. Self-funding is not the route for marginally financed entrepreneurs trying to save a buck. The risk of reneging on employee health claims for lack of cash is too great.

Consolidated Omnibus Budget Reconciliation Act (COBRA)

For firms with 20 or more employees, COBRA requires continuation of health benefits for workers and/or their dependents who would normally lose coverage due to the following specific qualifying events:

- Up to *18 months* of continuation is provided for those employees voluntarily or involuntarily terminated, or for those who lose health benefits because of reduction in hours, strikes, leave of absence, or layoffs.
- Up to *29 months* of coverage is extended to the disabled, under social security criteria.
- Up to *36 months* of continuation is provided for dependents of an employee who dies, is divorced or legally separated, or no longer qualifies as a dependent under the company health plan but is still legally claimed as a dependent under IRS tax regulations.

The employee has 60 days after the qualifying event to advise the company that he or she wishes to continue health benefits under COBRA coverage. Owners are not required to pay the group premium for the employee and may even charge an additional 2 percent to cover the administrative costs of the program. This 60-day period begins the date coverage is lost or the date notice is sent to the employee, whichever is later.

If continuation is elected by the employee or dependents, they have 45 days to pay the premium for retroactive benefits. Once the monthly payment cycle starts, they have a 30-day grace period each month to make the payments.

Note: COBRA can be a tricky item to administer. Make sure you get a complete copy of the regulations so you'll stay within the law. Although COBRA continuation means extra effort for the business owner, being able to maintain health insurance is a plus for employees leaving a company.

Disability Programs

Short-Term Disability Benefits (STD)

STD insurance provides salary continuation for employees who are temporarily disabled by injury or illnesses *not* related to work. Salary continuation for *work-related* injuries is covered under workers' compensation insurance.

Under STD programs, salary continuation can be for full pay or partial pay, with partial pay being the most common because experience has shown that with partial pay, employees will be motivated to return to work sooner. Under a partial pay plan, 60 percent of base pay is a standard amount. Some plans use length of service to determine how many weeks payments will continue. Other plans peg STD payments to a sliding scale, for example, 100 percent of pay for the first 30 days, 80 percent for the next 30 days, and 60 percent for the remaining period.

The majority of plans require a seven-day waiting period before benefits commence. During this period, employees should be able to use accrued but unused sick pay. The most popular STD plans cover up to 26 weeks (6 months) of compensation.

Note: California, Hawaii, New Jersey, New York, Rhode Island, and Puerto Rico mandate that employers carry STD insurance for non-work-related illnesses or injuries.

The majority of employers pay the full premium cost since premiums are not very expensive. Many employers self-insure their STD programs, paying out of current revenues as claims are incurred.

Long-Term Disability Programs (LTD)

LTD insurance provides salary continuation for employees who suffer extended illness or injury *not* related to the workplace. The waiting period for these benefits varies, with 180 days being a common choice. Benefit duration may extend to normal retirement age. Most smaller companies purchase LTD benefits from insurance companies. Because of risk, self-insurance is not common. Many companies require employee contributions via payroll deduction for premium costs.

Group Life Insurance

Group life insurance benefits are an important source of financial security for named beneficiaries in the event of the employee's death. The main types include the following:

- *Basic life insurance plans* cover the employee only, with the full premium normally paid by the employer. The benefit level may be the same for all employees or linked to a multiple of their annual salary, for example, one times the salary, two times the salary, and so forth.
- *Supplemental life insurance plans* provide additional insurance amounts with either the employer paying the full premium or sharing costs with the employee.
- *Dependent life insurance plans* provide benefits in the event of the death of an employee's spouse and/or children. Benefit payments for death of a spouse normally range between $5,000 and $10,000; for the death of a child, $2,000 to $5,000.

Accidental Death and Dismemberment (AD&D) Insurance

AD&D benefits provide a lump sum payment for accidental death. Similar to life insurance plans, the benefit amount is tied to annual salary. With the loss of eyes or limbs, lesser amounts are paid based on a percentage of the death benefit total. It is common to include both workplace and nonworkplace death or injury.

Flexible Spending Accounts (FSAs)

FSAs are tax-saving techniques that enable employees to set aside, via payroll deduction, tax-free dollars to cover qualified out-of-pocket health care expenses not paid by group insurance. Qualified expenses would include health plan deductibles and copayments.

Working with your accountant, individual employee accounts are established for those employees who voluntarily participate. The employee provides written authorization allowing the employer to deduct a specified pretax amount of gross wages. This amount is then deposited into that employee's flexible spending account.

As qualified expenses are incurred, the employee is reimbursed from money set aside in the FSA. Receipts showing proof of payment must be submitted by the employee. Unspent account balances, however, must be forfeited by the employee at the end of each year per IRS regulations. Often, employers sponsoring FSAs will contract with a third-party administrator to run the program.

Depending on the employee's income and other factors, FSAs may provide employee tax advantages. IRS publications 502 and 503 list eligible and ineligible expenses. In addition to health care expenses, certain employee dependent care expenses are also included in the FSA program.

Flexible spending accounts are really miniversions of cafeteria plans. For small businesses, experience with FSAs can prepare them for more sophisticated cafeteria plans if they grow large enough to need and support them.

Cafeteria Plans

Cafeteria plans are normally found in large corporations that have the money and technical support to run them. Most big firms have succeeded in providing all the core benefits and are in a position to install sophisticated programs to supplement them. Some feel compelled to do so for competitive reasons, wishing to be perceived by their employees and the public as having state-of-the-art benefits programs.

Cafeteria plans supplement basic core benefits. Both the employer and employee can contribute pretax dollars to individual flexible spending accounts. The money in these accounts can be used to purchase additional elective benefits such as added life insurance, dependent life insurance, deluxe health and dental benefit options, and richer disability insurance programs. Employees may earmark some of their account dollars for a 401(k) savings plan or take the money in cash. Some plans allow workers to sell back a portion of their vacation allotment to purchase other benefits.

Benefits Communication

An employer may provide excellent benefits but fail to communicate this fact to the employees, thereby losing valuable ground in employee relations. Firms that do provide good packages for their people should use every opportunity to tell them so. There is no reason to be shy. If this information is communicated properly, employees won't perceive the employer as boasting or bombarding them with self-serving propaganda.

Benefits professionals have confirmed through surveys that most employees are either unaware or don't fully understand their benefits packages. That's not too surprising since benefits can be a complicated subject. Younger employees don't understand their health benefits since few are or ever expect to get sick! Life insurance benefits won't hold much interest nor will dependent coverage if employees haven't started a family. Setting aside savings for retirement in the distant future with 401(k) plans may be furthest from their minds, yet their participation is needed to keep the plan balanced.

To be effective, benefits communication must be a continuing process that starts with the employment interview and ends with the exit interview or beyond if COBRA is in effect. With fewer people to contact, smaller businesses should be able to get the word out faster. The payroll person or an executive assistant can be assigned these communications duties. Educating employees can be done in a wide variety of ways including the following:

- *New employee orientation.* A good overview of the benefits package should be covered during these important sessions. It's an opportunity to discuss option choices, eligibility periods, plan limits and restrictions, and claim submission procedures. The better insurers should provide you with booklets and other support materials for your employees.

- *Employee meetings.* Hold meetings periodically to provide an overview of benefits, highlighting any changes or problems with the program. End with a question and answer session. If your staff is too busy, consider a learn-over-lunch meeting on a volunteer basis to go over benefits.

- *Employee handbook.* Include a benefits section in the handbook, highlighting benefits features.

- *Payroll stuffers.* Highlight benefit features on stuffers that are included in paycheck envelopes. If you have an outside payroll service, ask it to print a short message on your payroll vouchers regarding reenrollment sessions or other information.

- *Summary plan descriptions.* For health and welfare benefits and retirement savings plans ERISA law requires that employees have access to summary plan descriptions of these benefits.
- *Company newsletter.* Include a benefits section in your newsletter. Highlight a different benefit in each edition. When all benefits are covered, start the cycle again.
- *Letters to employee homes.* The employee may not have much interest in benefits, but perhaps a spouse, parents, or other family members will.

Other opportunities will present themselves for giving an employer a chance to educate employees on benefits, including contract renewal sessions when employees must reenroll and provide updated personal data to the insurer. Sick or injured employees may need information on coverage levels and claim submission procedures. The birth of a child or a divorce may be a good time to discuss dependent life insurance and update beneficiary designation forms.

Time Off Benefits

Pay for time not worked (sick leave, vacations, holidays) is often overlooked by the employer as an expense item. Often referred to as the hidden payroll, these costs can be substantial and should be taken into account in staff planning.

Paid Sick Days

Many small firms don't provide paid sick leave at all. They simply can't afford it. Remember though, paid sick leave does provide employees some level of financial security in the event of illness. It's also a basic benefit that helps to retain good people. Most programs provide a full day's pay when granting paid sick leave.

How many paid sick days you provide is really up to you. Barring a union-negotiated contract, you have flexibility. Your decision will depend on your own philosophy and what you think you can afford. Take into account what local competitors provide.

Paid sick day amounts can vary widely. For a smaller business, an amount anywhere within the 5 to 10 day per year range should take care of most noncritical, occasional illnesses. A safety net for longer temporary illnesses can be provided by adding a short-term disability program. You may decide to tie additional paid sick days to length of employment, with a cap. It is recommended that one approach be applied to all levels of employees.

Other factors to consider when establishing paid sick leave include the following:

- *Eligibility criteria.* For new employees the traditional practice is to activate paid sick leave programs only after they have met their initial employment period such as the first three or six months of employment. Often, management and/or other exempt employees are eligible for sick pay from their first day of employment.

- *Lump sum allotment.* Some firms make available to their employees the entire annual sick pay allotment on the first day of each new calendar year. Administratively, this is a simple approach. It may leave the company vulnerable, however, to those employees who plan to resign but wait until the new year to become eligible for a new sick leave allotment. They feign illness, use up their new allotment, and leave shortly thereafter.

- *Accrual approach.* This method accumulates sick leave on a monthly basis throughout the year until the full allotment is reached. For example, if 6 days are allowed per year, the employee would accrue one-half day each month over the 12-month period. If nine days are allowed, the monthly accrual would be three-quarters of a day each month. If the employee is out sick beyond the accrued allotment, no pay is extended for time taken beyond the accrued amount.

  Under the accrual system you may adopt a policy permitting the use of the full annual sick leave allotment early in the year, if needed. Employees terminating that year would then have any used but unaccrued sick pay deducted from their final paycheck.

- *Carryover policy.* This permits employees to carryover a portion of or all accrued but unused sick leave at the end of each year. In this way, the employee can bank paid sick days in case of extended illness. Often, caps are imposed limiting the amount that can be accumulated to the employee's carryover account.

- *Who is sick?* Many traditional sick pay programs were installed with just the employee's illness in mind. Often employees will call in sick but it is really a child or other family member who is ill. With the increase in dual career families and single parent households this trend will continue. You might consider extending legitimate illness to include immediate family members, particularly children.

No-Fault Absence

Some employers combine sick pay, personal days, and vacation benefits into one program. As with vacation days, the employee is entitled to take them during the year for any reason including illness. This eliminates the need to determine the legitimacy of sick days, which is a headache for owners and can cause friction with employees. For example, an employer has a traditional program that guarantees ten vacation days, six paid sick days, and three personal days per year. The sick days are to be taken only in the event of legitimate illness. The company moves to a no-fault plan that guarantees 15 paid absent days per year for whatever reason. Once these days are exhausted, no further pay is extended for absences during the remainder of the plan year. No-fault plans minimize police work for owners, and employees do not have to substantiate the occasional illness.

Paid Vacation Days

Just as with sick pay, you must determine how many paid vacation days you can afford and the standards within your industry. Traditional plans tie the vacation allotment to length of service with the company, for example, 10 days for the first 5 years of employment, 15 days for 6 to 14 years service, and so on. As with paid sick days, the accrual method can be used and eligibility can begin once a new employee gets through the initial employment period.

Part-Time Employees

If you employ part-time workers on a sustained basis, you may wish to provide them with paid vacation or sick days. A prorated approach can be taken, for example, if an employee's total weekly hours add up to half a normal workweek, give one-half of the annual first-year vacation or sick day allotment.

Paid Personal Days

These are paid days designated for personal reasons other than a normally scheduled vacation day or unanticipated sick day. Nonmedical appointments or emergencies are some examples. One or two days per year is the norm.

Paid Holidays

For those businesses not in retailing or other service industries, the seven traditional core holidays within the United States are the following:

New Year's Day	Labor Day
Presidents' Day	Thanksgiving Day
Memorial Day	Christmas Day
Independence Day	

Martin Luther King Jr.'s birthday is observed in many areas of the country, in many industries, and by government agencies. Good Friday is another observed holiday for some organizations. Companies with extended holiday programs will include the day after Thanksgiving, and the day before or after Christmas or New Year's, depending on which days of the week they fall each year.

The Floating Holiday

The concept of the floating holiday serves a useful purpose. Employees can use this day at any time during the calendar year for religious, cultural, or other observances. As our country becomes more ethnically and culturally diverse, the floating holiday is an effective means of addressing individual employee needs.

Work Breaks/Rest Periods (Nonexempt Employees)

Under the Fair Labor Standards Act (FLSA), you are *required* to pay for breaks or rest periods of 20 minutes or less. If you decide to provide rest breaks you must decide how many and of what duration. Remember, a scheduled 10- or 15-minute break usually ends up taking 20 minutes by the time everyone gets back into production.

Meal Periods (Nonexempt Employees)

Under FLSA, you *do not* have to pay for meal periods of 30 minutes or longer provided that employees are relieved of their duties and free to leave their workstation. Scheduled lunch hours for employees range between 30 and 60 minutes and most employers do not pay for lunch periods.

It is quite common to see employees decide to work through lunch hour, eating at their workstation. They may be very conscientious and wish to catch up or perhaps the weather outside is poor so they don't wish to go out.

Caution: It is important to remember that under FLSA, you are obligated to pay nonexempt employees for meal periods when they are not relieved of their duties. This is often overlooked by owners and employees. The practice may go on for years until one day a disgruntled employee reports it to the labor department, demanding back pay and prompting a wage and hour audit. Fines and awards of back wages may result.

Other Types of Paid Leave

The employee's birthday. If it falls on a workday, he or she gets the day off with pay.

Employee's anniversary date with the company. If it falls on a workday, provide the day off with pay.

Marriage week. Provide one additional week with pay for an employee's marriage. (If you choose to provide such a benefit, expect some employees to request a paid divorce week as well.)

Bereavement days. Up to three days is recommended for the death of immediate family members including spouse, children, parents, brothers and sisters, and grandparents. Less may be provided for other relatives such as aunts, uncles, and in-laws.

Jury duty. Jurors receive pay for their services from the court system. Will you deduct the difference employees receive from jury service from their paychecks or ask them to endorse the jury service check over to the company if you continued full pay? Or will you allow them to enjoy full company pay in addition to jury pay as a perk for performing a community service?

Military leave. As with jury service, will you continue full pay for those on military leave? The law does not require you to do so. Normally, pay is provided for the two-week annual reserve training.

Guidelines for Entrepreneurs and Small Business Owners

Employee Benefits

The smaller businesses usually can't afford to provide much in the way of employee benefits. For many, just meeting social security, workers' compensation, and unemployment insurance payments is tough enough. Providing health insurance for their employees may simply be out of the question. Just as with base wages, owners are limited by what they can afford.

- For any business, health insurance is the premier benefit to have. If you can afford it, great. Even a basic program will help in attracting and retaining employees.
- Owners don't have to carry the entire group health insurance cost on their own. Premium sharing with the employee is the norm today. Combined with higher deductibles and copayments, you might be able to afford a reasonable group plan for your workers.
- Managed care health programs seem to be proving the least expensive approach to take with health care insurance plans.
- Time off benefits are important as well, particularly for working parents who can really use this time to care for their children.
- Flexibility in taking time off is also important, so consider the no-fault absence approach. Keep in mind, however, that the needs of the business must come first.

8

SAVINGS, RETIREMENT, AND INCENTIVE PROGRAMS

This chapter provides a brief overview of popular programs that enable employees to save for retirement as well as earn additional compensation beyond their base wages. Included are the main types of retirement plans and various incentive award programs that give employees the opportunity to earn extra money through higher productivity.

A balance must be struck between how much money is spent on employee benefits and how much on cash compensation. Maintaining this balance is a continuing process. When administering cash compensation programs remember that the more wages you pay, the higher your mandated benefits costs will be, such as the company social security match, unemployment, and workers' compensation costs. Higher cash compensation will also affect the cost of certain benefits programs. Life insurance premiums may rise if coverage levels are linked to an employee's annual salary.

Short- and long-term disability benefits are commonly linked to a percentage of base wages. As wages rise, so will the insurer's liability for greater disability payments. This exposure may be reflected in higher premiums at renewal.

SAVINGS AND RETIREMENT PROGRAMS

Two main categories of pension plans currently exist in our society: defined benefit plans and defined contribution plans.

Defined Benefit Pension Plans

Defined benefit plans are designed to *guarantee* retiring employees with a fixed percentage of their final average salary at retirement, for example, 50 to 60 percent. This fixed percentage is known or defined up front, years before actual retirement. Employer money must be invested each year to ensure that enough dollars are available to fund the employee's retirement at this guaranteed percentage. Actuaries reestimate the dollars needed annually to fund this obligation.

In today's business climate fewer defined benefit plans are being installed by companies. They involve heavy administrative expenses, adherence to extensive government regulations under the Employee Retirement Income Security Act (ERISA), and incur financial obligations few firms are willing to take these days.

These plans were designed to encourage employees to remain with the company for their entire working careers, reflecting a more stable economic environment. Rapid technological change, corporate downsizing, and international competition have substantially eroded this environment. Few new defined benefits plans are being established today by the big companies and fewer still for small businesses.

Defined Contribution Pension Plans

Defined contribution plans don't guarantee any fixed level of income when an employee retires. They do, however, define a fixed amount of company contributions that are to be made each year toward the employee's retirement. This money is invested, and both gains and losses are credited to the employee's account. The retirement benefit is whatever is in this account at the time of retirement. *Note:* Defined contribution plans can also be written to include employee contributions as well.

Defined contribution plans are the most popular choice today. Although still subject to government rules and regulation, the financial risks and administrative burdens are much less than for defined benefit plans. Defined contribution plans include the following:

1. 401(k) Plans

401(k)s have become the mainstay for small and midsize companies that wish to provide a means for employees to accumulate retirement income. They are popular with larger corporations as well, but generally as a supplement to existing defined benefit or defined contribution pension plans.

The pretax advantage. The government, in its attempt to encourage retirement savings, has permitted employers to sponsor 401(k) plans. These plans enable employees to apportion a fixed percentage of their paycheck as savings on a pretax basis, before most withholding taxes are deducted. The money is deposited into a trust account with a bank or other financial services company for investment purposes.

Account balances are maintained separately for each participating employee and investment earnings are sheltered from taxation, enabling savings to compound at an accelerated rate. Regulatory restrictions and penalties exist for withdrawals made prior to retirement.

Highly compensated employees. 401(k) regulations are written to encourage savings for the mid- and lower-level employee. Regulatory controls exist to prevent highly compensated employees from saving proportionately more money than the nonhighly compensated. To offset an imbalance, adjustments may be required to lower the contribution percentages for highly paid people, or refund portions of their savings. It may even be necessary for the company to contribute money to nonhighly compensated employee accounts in order to maintain the required balance.

Many employers make matching contributions, based on a preselected formula, to enhance employee participation. Others permit after-tax employee contributions to be made. Plans can also be written to allow for employee loans.

Consider the nature of your business and earnings level of your employees before sponsoring a 401(k) plan. Companies employing predominantly lower-paid workers may have difficulty sustaining a plan. Lower-paid employees have less to save or may be unwilling to live with the restrictions on premature withdrawals. Firms with high turnover may encounter problems as well.

2. Money Purchase Plans

The employer invests money based on a fixed percentage of an employee's base salary. The company invests this money in insurance annuities which provide the employee with a fixed annual income upon retirement.

3. Deferred Profit Sharing Plan

The business contributes a percentage of its profits each year to be credited to individual employee investment accounts. The money itself is placed in an outside trust account with a bank or other financial institution for safeguarding and investment. Investment gains and losses are allocated back to individual employee accounts on a prorated basis calculated using a predetermined formula. The retirement benefit is whatever amount is in the account when the employee retires. *Note:* If no profits are made by the company in any one year, no contributions are made to the individual employee accounts. Profits sharing plans do have some incentive value for employees, however, profits are also influenced by outside market conditions which can cause losses beyond an organization's control.

EMPLOYEE INCENTIVE PROGRAMS

Enrich the eagles, feed the pigeons, starve the turkeys.
—Peter V. Le Blanc, at an ACA Seminar, Oct. 1993

Incentive programs provide additional compensation to eligible employees beyond their base wage. They are designed to motivate employees to make greater efforts for the company. Businesses are realizing that base pay alone is often insufficient for stimulating workers to put forth the efforts required in today's marketplace. Base pay may be very effective in providing a fair wage and attracting good workers, yet have little impact on encouraging them to go above and beyond the line of duty on a continuing basis.

Some awards programs have been around for years, particularly in manufacturing environments. Others are fairly new or in the experimental stages at the bigger companies that can better afford the costs and mistakes associated with new programs. Most are custom designed to fit the specific needs of the organization. The more elaborate programs require sustained support from top management because of the time they require to install and maintain.

The following programs are covered in this section.

1. Individual cash awards
2. Sales commission plans
3. Annual bonus plans
4. Group bonus plans
5. Stock bonus plans
6. Stock compensation plans
7. Variable pay programs
8. Skill-based pay
9. Perquisites or perks

You may have opportunities to experiment with some of these programs, starting small and proceeding cautiously until satisfied with the results. Avoid installing another company's program piecemeal. The elements contributing to success in one company may not be present in your own organization. The staff, financial assets, and business operation may be completely different.

Program Objectives

Prior to considering alternative award programs take the time to clarify your objectives. What do you wish to accomplish within your own business? Will the program be compatible with your performance review system, if you have one in place, or will adjustments have to be made?

Clarifying which employee behaviors you wish to encourage is a basic step in designing your own program. Traditional incentive objectives include the following:

- *Cost control.* If reducing business expenses is a high priority take a look at your budget line items and decide which areas deserve the most attention. These may range from reducing material waste to holding the line on staff additions.
- *Quality control.* Is quality essential to your business? If so, can an increase in quality be measured and used to support incentive awards?
- *Speed of production.* If you run a processing type of operation, can you speed up throughput by a certain percentage without hurting quality or overworking your people? Again, can you measure results?
- *Improvements.* All business operations can be improved. Can yours be improved to such a degree that you can identify good results? Are you strong on encouraging your workers to continually strive to improve their operations?
- *Teamwork.* Because of foreign competition, particularly with Japan, much has been written on employee teamwork. The results of teamwork or simple employee cooperation can improve operations dramatically.
- *Customer service.* This is another concept that is getting much attention today. The challenge is how to measure and reward good customer service well enough to establish an incentive program. Spot cash awards or gifts to employees who receive frequent customer praise is one approach to consider.
- *Safety.* This is a major concern in industries with traditionally high accident rates. The cost of workers' compensation and Occupational Safety and Health Administration (OSHA) compliance can be substantial as can the more obvious problems of lost production and employee welfare.

Individual Cash Awards

Cash awards for individual performance are quite popular because most people can relate to the concept of getting additional money for extra effort. Cash in addition to the regular wage is awarded when specific production or project goals are achieved. One of the oldest forms of individual incentive is commissions paid to salespersons.

Effective programs have a short cycle time between the desired performance and cash award, for example, quarterly payouts. Participating employees also have a clear line of sight to the targeted performance and are able to reasonably control the conditions required to succeed and earn more money.

Plan specifics and goal standards should be communicated to employees in writing. Include a plan expiration date (sunset clause) to avoid having the program be considered an entitlement. Program review is essential because changes in operations may affect how hard or easy it is to meet the plan's goals.

Sales Commission Plans

Salespersons are normally paid a specific percentage of gross sales for products or services they sell. Base wages may or may not be paid, depending upon the industry. In order to provide income during slack periods, many plans enable the salesperson to draw (borrow) money from the employer against future anticipated commissions.

Annual Bonus Plans

Annual company bonuses are often paid out during the year-end holiday season. The amount is discretionary, determined each year by the owner. Different payout criteria are used including a lump sum payment based on a set percentage of base salary. Newer employees may be given less or excluded altogether. The incentive value of these plans is minimal, since most are not closely linked to individual employee or unit performance.

Group Bonus Plans

Entrepreneurs seeking to encourage group effort may award additional money in the form of a bonus if production targets are met. Employees eligible for such programs normally work in a definable group with common goals and functions. They must depend on and cooperate with one another to achieve defined results. In designing such plans owners must be sure that the group has reasonable control over the forces that determine success. Outside conditions or even internal forces beyond their control can undermine such programs.

Gainsharing is a type of group bonus plan. Employees within specified working groups share with the company dollars saved through productivity gains. Performance is measured against historical standards, and savings in production costs are converted to cash payouts. These plans can be quite effective and reinforce the concept of workers as team players. Normally group effort and cooperation are required for positive results.

Stock Bonus Plans

Stock ownership plans award employees company stock if certain profit or productivity measures are achieved. Stock plans presuppose that employees with an ownership interest will identify more closely with the organization. Employees may also be allowed to purchase stock at discount prices.

Stock Compensation Plans

Eligible employees, usually officers, are given part of their regular compensation in the form of company stock rather than cash. Earning an ownership interest in a company can be a powerful incentive for higher performance.

Variable Pay Programs

Also called pay-at-risk programs, variable pay has attracted much publicity in recent years. Similar to the compensation approach used for some sales jobs, management employees are guaranteed a base wage somewhat below market rates. They must earn any additional compensation by meeting defined production targets or other objectives. Cash rewards substantially above market rates are available to those demonstrating outstanding levels of performance. Variable pay can be an excellent motivator for people who can sustain high levels of achievement on a consistent basis and are strongly motivated to make money.

Skill-Based Pay

The basis for skill-based pay programs is that employees can earn more by learning more. Additional pay is awarded when they demonstrate mastery of new job-related skills or a body of knowledge. The objective is to develop and retain a highly skilled workforce. These plans require clearly defined skill levels and the employee must have the opportunity to acquire the new skills either on the job or with outside training paid by the company.

Perquisites or Perks

The need for status has always been a part of the human condition and organizations have capitalized on this for centuries. Normally, perks are awarded to higher management people based on their position and rarely on performance. Perks can be very effective in supporting traditional organization structures and are used to define the management as separate from the workers. The use of perks is declining somewhat or at least being deemphasized. Organizations wishing to encourage teamwork and worker participation avoid them.

Popular perks include reserved parking spaces, country and health club memberships, private dining and restrooms for upper management, company cars and cellular phones, and first-class accommodations on airliners.

Guidelines for Entrepreneurs and Small Business Owners

Savings, Retirement, and Incentive Programs

- Firms with only a few people usually have no employee savings or retirement plans in place; participation would not be large enough to warrant the administrative expense. Opportunities for incentive programs, however, do exist. These programs usually take the form of a holiday bonus or spot cash awards for meeting specific goals.

- Once appropriate goals are selected, it is important to have accurate measures of performance. Employees should also have reasonable control of results.

- For the larger firm with over 100 employees, 401(k) plans are becoming the savings and retirement plan of choice. Employees are increasingly expected to save more for their own retirement, with the company helping with matching funds up to a specified percentage of savings.

9

LEGAL ISSUES

It's no secret that compliance with employment laws has become a major challenge for the business community. In our society, entrepreneurs have been made responsible for a host of societal and economic activities far beyond the traditional role of operating for profit. Following are some examples:

- The wage withholding laws have made owners into tax collectors for federal, state, and local governments.
- Garnishment and domestic court order laws involve owners in the collection of workers' personal debts.
- Under child labor legislation, companies share in the responsibility of affording safety and protection to minors.
- The Family Medical Leave Act has committed employers to a larger role in the personal lives of their employees.
- Under the Consolidated Omnibus Budget Reconciliation Act (COBRA), owners who sponsor health insurance benefits

must now maintain insurance coverage (at employee expense), for workers no longer in their employ.

- Under civil rights legislation, employers bear the bulk of society's responsibility for addressing past and present discrimination. Interestingly enough, Congress has only recently allowed itself to be subject to these laws.

- Via immigration legislation, employers share responsibility for controlling illegal immigration with the Immigration and Naturalization Service.

If past legislative trends are an indicator, you can expect even more legislation in the future.

Figure 9-1 provides an overview of how federal employment legislation applies to entrepreneurs who employ only a few people.

Before moving on to federal legislation it is important to remember that state employment laws also play their role in regulating employers. Often, state laws are similar to their federal counterparts or provide more comprehensive coverage and benefits for covered employees. In such cases the state law may apply, taking precedence over the federal equivalent.

Your attorney or local state Department of Labor are sources for copies of state employment laws. Another option is to purchase or subscribe to commercial publications specializing in employment law information. A good example is Business & Legal Reports, Inc. (BLR). BLR produces a series entitled *What to Do About Personnel Problems in (your state)*. In addition to covering various personnel topics, the publication indicates the state laws that apply to those topics. Updates are mailed periodically for insertion in the series binder. Cost is approximately $300 for an annual subscription. Federal law is included as well. If you have employees in more than one state, BLR produces the *Quick Guide to Employment Law* which covers state laws in all 50 states. It costs about $150. Call or write for their catalogs: Business & Legal Reports, Inc., 39 Academy Street, Madison, CT 06443-1513, Tel: 800-727-5257.

The rest of this chapter provides an overview of the most common federal and state civil laws regulating the employer-employee relationship:

Figure 9-1   Reference Guide to Legislation

Quick Reference Guide to Federal Employment Legislation

Legislation	Coverage Threshold
Age Discrimination in Employment Act (ADEA) Prohibits age discrimination in employment for persons age 40 and over	Employers with 20 or more employees
Americans with Disabilities Act of 1990 Prohibits discrimination in employment against qualified individuals with disabilities	Employers with 15 or more employees
Civil Rights Act of 1991 Provides for compensatory and punitive damages in cases of intentional discrimination. For employers with 15 to 100 employees, fines are capped at $50,000.	Employers with 15 or more employees
Civil Rights Act of 1964-Title VII Prohibits discrimination against workers or applicants because of race, color, religion, sex, or national origin	Employers with 15 or more employees
Consolidated Omnibus Budget Reconciliation Act (COBRA) Provides for continuation of company-sponsored health insurance benefits for terminated employees and their qualified dependents at employee's expense	Employers sponsoring health plans with 20 or more employees
Davis-Bacon Act Specifies that prevailing wages and fringe benefits must be paid by businesses primarily doing government construction contracts	Employers with federal contracts exceeding $2,500
Employee Polygraph Protection Act of 1988 Specifies restrictions of employment lie detector tests	Most employers
Employment Retirement Income Security Act (ERISA) Rules and regulations covering employer-sponsored pension, retirement, and health and welfare plans	Employers who sponsor qualified pension, health, and welfare plans
Equal Pay Act (EPA) Prohibits wage discrimination based on sex	Employers with 2 or more employees

(continued)

Figure 9-1   *Continued*

Executive Order 11246—Affirmative Action Specifies written affirmative action plans	Employers with federal contracts exceeding $50,000 and 50 or more employees
Fair Labor Standards Act (FLSA) Specifies minimum wage, overtime regulations, and child labor restrictions	Most employers
Federal Insurance Contributions Act (FICA) Social Security Tax Law	Most employers
Federal Unemployment Tax Act (FUTA) Unemployment Tax Law	Employers with one or more employees working over 20 different calendar weeks and making $1,500 or more during any quarter
Immigration Reform and Control Act of 1986 (IRCA) Prohibits the hiring of persons not authorized to work in the United States	All employers
Labor-Management Relations Act of 1947 (Taft-Hartley) Provides ground rules for employees and employers during union-organizing campaigns	All employers engaging in interstate commerce
The Occupational Safety and Health Act of 1970 Outlines duties of employers to protect employees from work related hazards	Most employers
Rehabilitation Act of 1973 Prohibits discrimination against the handicapped	Employers with federal contracts or subcontracts exceeding $2,500
The Family Medical Leave Act of 1993 (FMLA) Entitles employees to up to 12 weeks unpaid leave for employee- or family-related illness or care	Employers with 50 or more employees
Vietnam Era Veterans Readjustment Assistance Act Requires written affirmative action programs to hire Vietnam veterans	Employers with federal contracts and 50 or more employees
Walsh-Healy Act Covers wage rates for federal contractors supplying goods and equipment to the government	Employers with federal contracts exceeding $10,000
Worker Adjustment and Retraining Notification Act (WARN) Required 60 days' advance written warning of major layoffs	Employers with 100 or more employees

1. Wage and hour laws
2. Civil rights employment laws
3. Other employment-related laws
4. Laws applying to employee benefits
5. Laws involving federal contracts or federally funded contracts
6. Labor laws dealing primarily with union relations
7. State civil laws that can affect employers

WAGE AND HOUR LAWS

The following laws are mentioned in this section:

Law	Company Is Covered If It Has
Federal and State Unemployment Tax Acts (FUTA, SUTA)	1 employee
Federal Insurance Contributions Act (FICA)	1 employee
Fair Labor Standards Act (FLSA)	1 employee

For business owners, it is amazing how fast each payday approaches. In both good and bad times the payroll is with you. Receivables may be slow coming in, but payday always arrives right on time! Employees eagerly anticipate their paycheck, often taking great pains in analyzing their withholding statements. Owners or their payroll clerks are quickly challenged if one penny is missing.

New business owners often underestimate the time it may take to educate and explain basic wage and hours laws to their people. Good communication over payroll is probably one of the most important employee relations techniques, yet it is often overlooked. Many employees don't fully understand how their employer arrived at their net pay, particularly those new to the workforce. What they don't understand they'll often mistrust, feeling that somehow they're being cheated.

Income Tax, Social Security, and Unemployment Insurance

If you don't have the time or expertise, ask your accountant to come in and hold an orientation session with your people about the following:

- Explain federal and state income tax withholding forms, exemptions, and dependent allowances.
- FICA means Federal Insurance Contributions Act. It authorizes taxes to support the social security and medicare programs. The employer must match the employee deduction with an additional 7.65 percent.
- FUTA means Federal Unemployment Tax Act, and SUTA applies to state unemployment taxes. Both are used to fund unemployment benefits.
- Explain deductions for employee contributions to health insurance and other benefits.

Note: It is not uncommon for smaller businesses having cash flow problems to delay making required employment tax deposits. This is a dangerous practice and not unknown to state and federal tax authorities. Back taxes can build quickly, with penalties or fines imposed when the shortfall is discovered.

Fair Labor Standards Act of 1938 (FLSA)

This act covers minimum wage and overtime regulations for nonexempt workers. It defines the workweek, training wages, and child labor restrictions for workers under the age of 18. It also defines the exempt and nonexempt classifications which are covered in more detail in Chapter 2.

The basic law has been on the books for over 50 years. Passed during the Great Depression, the federal government is currently assessing its usefulness in our modern era. Over time, FLSA has become much too restrictive for businesses and employees alike. Changes are in order to add more flexibility for both business owners and employees.

Misclassification of Independent Contractors

Over the years many companies have attempted to avoid paying payroll taxes by misclassifying employees as independent contractors. Other firms just don't understand what constitutes an independent contractor. They may be paying people as contractors when they are really considered employees by the IRS. Both the IRS and state tax authorities have recently intensified their auditing activities in this area and are collecting millions in back taxes and fines.

What constitutes an independent contractor? This may not be easily answered as gray areas exist in the law. The IRS has multiple criteria that they use during audits. Different weight is given to each criterion depending upon the individual circumstances within the company under investigation. If you do bring in outside help, play it safe and ensure that you comply with the following:

- Check that the person does indeed have his or her own business, with business tax ID number, business cards, business liability insurance if needed, and any necessary business licenses.
- Ask for a list of current or prior clients.
- Make sure that your company is not the only client or primary source of income.
- Get in writing a list of the services to be performed and estimated costs.
- Don't control the sequence or the order of the work performed.
- Don't provide significant administrative or other help to enable the person to perform the task.
- Make sure the person can hire his or her own help and pay them out of the business.
- Don't supply the tools and equipment to do the job.
- Don't pay the person's travel or business expenses.
- Don't provide any staff perks or benefits.
- Don't set hours of work for the person.
- Don't train the person how to do the work.
- Don't pay the person out of the normal payroll account.

Federal and State Wage Assignment Laws (Garnishments)

Garnishment is where, upon receipt of a court order, employers are required to make deductions from an employee's disposable earnings to cover debts to creditors. Disposable earnings are what's left after deductions for income and social security taxes. Garnishment laws cover all employers.

Under the federal law, the garnished amount may not exceed 25 percent of the disposable earnings in any one workweek. Special restrictions are applicable for child support orders. The federal law prohibits an employer from discharging any employee because his earnings have been subject to garnishment for any one indebtedness.

When processing garnishments be sure to retain strict confidentiality. The employee's privacy is at stake. With the exception of the employee, only those involved in processing the payroll have a need to know. The company may be held liable for the money owed by its employee if it fails to make the required withholdings.

CIVIL RIGHTS EMPLOYMENT LAWS

The following laws are covered in this section:

Law	Company Is Covered If It Has
Civil Rights Act of 1964—Title VII	15 employees
Civil Rights Act of 1991 (CRA)	15 employees
The Age Discrimination in Employment Act (ADEA)	20 employees
The Equal Pay Act (EPA)	2 employees
The Americans with Disabilities Act (ADA)	15 employees

For a small firm with limited cash reserves, losing a civil rights suit can be serious. Even if you win, legal defense costs can be substantial. There are cases in which plaintiffs have sued owners and managers *personally*, as well as the company.

Many states have their own equal employment opportunity enforcement agencies known as Fair Employment Practice Agencies (FEPAs). Because of massive case backlogs in both federal and state enforcement agencies, interest in **alternative dispute resolution (ADR)** is on the rise within the business community and government. The mediation and arbitration techniques used to resolve management and union disputes are now being applied to nonunion situations. ADR is faster and less expensive than outside litigation. The practice is growing and good results are being reported, so it's a trend worth watching.

Civil Rights Act of 1964—Title VII

A major civil rights law, Title VII prohibits employers with 15 or more employees from discriminating against workers or job applicants because of race, color, religion, sex, or national origin. This law is not limited to just hiring or termination. It covers other terms and conditions of employment such as possible discrimination in compensation, assignment, or classification of employees; transfers, promotion, layoff, or recall; job advertisements, recruitment, testing, use of company facilities, and training and apprenticeship programs; fringe benefits, retirement plans, and disability leave.

Civil Rights Act of 1991 (CRA)

The CRA provides for compensatory and punitive damages in cases of intentional discrimination. Damage amounts relate to company size and are capped as follows:

- 15–100 employees: $50,000
- 101–200 employees: $100,000
- 201–500 employees: $200,000
- More than 500 employees: $300,000

The Civil Rights Act of 1991 also provides for jury trials, which is bad news for employers, particularly large companies with deep pockets. Historically, employers don't fair well with juries. A decade of corporate layoffs and early retirements has made many people available to serve on juries. You can imagine where their sympathy will lie.

Sexual Harassment

National television coverage of famous sexual harassment cases has sensitized the public to this issue. Sexual harassment cases evolved from the Civil Rights Act of 1964. Sexual harassment in the workplace has been defined as **unwelcome** activity of a sexual nature when one or more of the following applies:

- Acceptance or rejection of the conduct is used to make employment decisions (hiring, promotion, work assignments, and pay increases).
- The conduct has the purpose or effect of unreasonably interfering with job performance.
- The conduct creates an intimidating, hostile, or offensive work environment.

The conduct does not have to be sexual in nature. Cruel treatment directed only at women can be the basis for action. Male owners who use their power to abuse and belittle only female employees is an example. An employer can also be held liable for sexual harassment conducted by coworkers and nonemployees such as customers, outside salespeople, and other visitors.

The Investigation

Once brought to management's attention, reports of sexual harassment require prompt and thorough investigation despite the potential for embarrassment and controversy. A sincere, well-documented attempt to resolve the issue is a strong defense if your company is sued later on and must defend itself in court.

Sexual harassment complaints are highly emotional matters, so be sensitive when interviewing the involved parties, including any witnesses. Ensure the investigation includes only those directly involved in the incident, including witnesses. Confidentiality is critical not only to protect the parties involved, but also to protect the company from a possible lawsuit.

The following should be included in an investigation of sexual harassment:

- Interview the person who made the complaint.
- Interview those accused.

- Interview witnesses.

When interviewing the person complaining of being harassed, take good notes and get all the facts surrounding the complaint, including the following:

- The time, place, and date of the incident. If more than one is reported, keep separate notes on each occurrence.
- What specifically was the behavior that caused the complaint? If it was verbal abuse, what was said; if it was touching, what part of the body was touched and by whom?
- Were there any witnesses to the incident? If so, who?
- How did the person complaining react to the alleged harassment? What was said or done? Was it reported to a supervisor? Was this the first time? Was it kidding around that got out of hand?
- What does the person feel should be done by management to resolve the situation?

When interviewing the person accused of the sexual harassment, be mindful that perceptions and degrees of what constitutes sexual harassment can differ greatly from person to person. Be prepared for a denial of the accusation. Those accused may express shock or dismay, claiming they were only joking or teasing the employee claiming the harassment.

- Explain the nature of the complaint to the accused, including time, dates, and what occurred.
- Allow the accused to make a statement regarding the accusation, again, taking good notes of what is said.
- Don't make quick judgments; you are gathering facts at this stage.
- What was the person's relationship to the one who has complained?
- What does the accused feel should be done to resolve the incident?

Good, reliable witnesses can help substantiate the validity of the complaint. Again, get their statements and interpretations of what occurred. Without witnesses, the problem may be harder to resolve because the situation becomes one person's word against another's.

If you have enough information to confirm that harassment took place, prompt disciplinary action is required. If the matter is not too serious, a written warning, with a copy to the personnel file may be all that's needed. Be sure to warn the harasser of the seriousness of the matter and that further behavior of this nature may result in termination. Also explain that the harasser can also be charged personally in a court of law for his or her actions.

More serious matters may require suspension, a demotion in rank, or termination of employment. Carefully document any warnings or other disciplinary action taken to resolve the issue.

If you cannot determine guilt or innocence, you may wish to contact your attorney to do a more detailed investigation. If this is impractical, be sure to explain to both parties involved in the incident that although you were unable to reach a definite conclusion in the investigation, you don't take sexual harassment matters lightly. Keep detailed records of the investigation and results. Having this documentation may help substantiate your good faith effort in reacting quickly to the complaint if a lawsuit is filed later.

The atmosphere in the workplace can be the spawning ground for sexual harassment problems, particularly in traditionally male-dominated businesses. How employees behave may very well depend on what the owner will tolerate. Allowing sexy magazines and calendars on the premises or permitting risqué banter in the presence of the opposite sex is an invitation to trouble. There are many good training programs designed to prevent sexual harassment in the workplace. Consider bringing in an outside educator to train anyone in a supervisory role.

The Age Discrimination in Employment Act (ADEA)

The ADEA covers persons 40 years old and over. This law prohibits age discrimination in hiring, discharge, pay, promotions, fringe benefits, and other aspects of employment. It applies to private employers of 20 or more workers. Charges have increased dramatically in recent years because of corporate downsizings.

The Equal Pay Act (EPA)

The EPA prohibits employers from discriminating on the basis of sex in the payment of wages in situations where men and women perform substantially equal work under similar working conditions in the same establishment. The law does not apply to pay differences based on factors such as seniority, merit, or systems that determine wages based upon the quantity or quality of items produced or processed.

The Americans with Disabilities Act (ADA)

The ADA covers employers with 15 or more workers (as of July 26, 1994). The law prohibits discrimination in employment against qualified individuals with disabilities. A qualified individual with a disability is a person who meets legitimate skill, experience, education, or other job requirements and who can perform the essential functions of the position with or without reasonable accommodation.

Reasonable Accommodation

Reasonable accommodation is any modification by an employer that will enable people with disabilities to apply for a job or perform its essential functions if hired. Examples include the following:

- Making existing facilities accessible to a person with a disability, for example, installing ramps and renovating rest rooms or workstations to accommodate those requiring wheel chairs
- Where possible, adjusting parts of the job to allow for the disability
- Modifying work schedules
- Acquiring or changing equipment
- Providing qualified readers for the visually impaired
- Modifying examinations or training programs for the visually or hearing impaired

According to the Equal Employment Opportunity Commission, reasonable accommodation also includes "... adjustments to assure that a qualified individual with a disability has rights and privileges in employment equal to those of non-disabled employees."

Note: The intent of the ADA is to enable disabled persons to compete in the workplace *without* eroding performance standards.

Who Is Considered Disabled?

An individual is considered to have a disability if that person has a mental or physical impairment that restricts one or more major life activities. Major examples are impairments that affect hearing, seeing, and speaking; walking and breathing; learning; and caring for oneself. Individuals with epilepsy, paralysis, HIV infection, AIDS, a substantial mental retardation, or a specific learning disability, to name just a few, are included. In addition, those with a record of a disability, such as a person who has recovered from cancer or mental illness, and individuals who are regarded as having some sort of impairment even if they really don't have one at all can be considered disabled.

Since its effective date in July 1992, this law has caused quite a bit of confusion and consternation among employers of all kinds and sizes. Gray areas exist in understanding the meaning and degree of disability. New interpretations can be expected with the increasing number of discrimination lawsuits being filed under this act.

Civil Rights Charges

In Title VII cases, charging parties have 180 days after the alleged discrimination takes place to file suit with the Equal Employment Opportunity Commission (EEOC). In many states, a state agency or Fair Employment Practice Agency (FEPA) may handle the claim. The EEOC will defer the claim to the state, even providing money to help defray state costs.

If the person filing charges against the company is still employed there, owners should be very careful on how they react. Getting angry and firing the person can result in a second lawsuit claiming illegal retaliation for exercising the individual's rights under the law.

The EEOC (or state agency) will interview the charging party to obtain as much information as possible and, if all legal jurisdiction requirements are met, to file the charge with the employer. In investigating the charge to determine if discrimination occurred, the EEOC requests information from the employer. This includes copies of personnel files if required.

Any witnesses who have direct knowledge of the alleged discrimination will be interviewed. If the evidence shows there is no cause to believe discrimination occurred, this should close the matter. If reasonable cause for discrimination is found, the EEOC will first attempt to persuade the employer to voluntarily eliminate and remedy the discrimination through conciliation. Remedies may include the following:

- Back pay
- Restoration of lost benefits, and damages to compensate for actual monetary loss
- Limited monetary damages to pay for future monetary loss, mental anguish, or pain and suffering, and to penalize any owner who acted with malice or reckless indifference
- Requiring the employer to post a notice in the workplace advising employees that it has complied with orders to remedy the discrimination

If all attempts at conciliation fail the Equal Employment Opportunity Commission can file a lawsuit in federal district court on behalf of the person suing the company. It may take a year or more before the actual hearing is scheduled and additional years before a case is resolved. The employee, unless engaging a personal attorney, incurs very little expense when filing a civil rights charge, however, the emotional costs can be high for both the employer and the employee particularly if the employee is still employed by the organization.

At the time of this writing, the EEOC has over 100,000 cases pending. FEPAs have approximately 60,000 cases. Not all of these cases are valid. Unfortunately, the system is being choked with many cases having no real merit.

Note: The EEOC provides a free booklet outlining the text of these important laws in more depth. Ask for a copy of *Laws Enforced by the U.S. Equal Employment Opportunity Commission.* Write to the Office of Communications and Legislative Affairs, EEOC, 1801 L St., NW, Washington, DC 20507.

OTHER EMPLOYMENT-RELATED LAWS

The following laws are covered in this section:

Law	Company Is Covered If It Has
The Immigration Reform and Control Act of 1986 (IRCA)	1 employee
The Family and Medical Leave Act of 1993 (FMLA)	50 employees
Worker Adjustment and Retraining Notification Act (WARN)	100 employees
Employee Polygraph Protection Act of 1988	1 employee
The Occupational Safety and Health Act of 1970	1 employee

The Immigration Reform and Control Act of 1986 (IRCA)

The IRCA law prohibits hiring persons not authorized to work in the United States. It also prohibits discriminating against noncitizens who do have authorization to work in the United States. Employers must see specific documents verifying a new employee's identity and eligibility to work in this country. The completion of the Employment Eligibility Verification Form (I-9) is a part of this verification process.

The Immigration and Naturalization Service (INS) publishes a handbook for completing this important form. Entitled *Handbook For Employees*, it contains sample I-9 forms that can be copied, as well as information on complying with the law. Contact your local

INS office for a copy of the handbook and a limited number of I-9 forms.

The Family and Medical Leave Act of 1993 (FMLA)

The FMLA covers employers with 50 or more employees. It entitles employees to take up to 12 weeks of unpaid leave per year for any of the following reasons:

- The birth of a child and to care for the newborn child
- The placement of a child with the employee for adoption or foster care
- Caring for a family member (child, spouse, or parent) with a serious health condition
- A personal, serious health condition that makes the employee unable to perform the functions of his or her job

Employers covered by the law are required to maintain any preexisting group health coverage during the leave period and, once the leave period is over, reinstate the employee to the same or equivalent job, with equivalent employment benefits, pay, and other terms and conditions of employment.

Congress's intent in passing the act was to foster a better balance between work and family needs. Compliance so far has not proved simple, particularly among big firms with large numbers of employees. Accurately keeping track of intermittent leave days can be difficult.

The following are some of the important points of the law:

- *Employer eligibility.* The law applies to any business employing 50 or more employees for 20 or more calendar weeks within a 75-mile radius.
- *Employee eligibility.* Eligible employees include those with at least 12 months of service with the company and 1,250 hours of working time during that period.
- *Serious health condition of an employee.* This means an illness, injury, or physical or mental condition requiring inpatient

hospital care and continuing treatment by a health care provider.

- *Intermittent and reduced leave schedules.* Leaves may be taken in separate segments (e.g., so many hours per workday). A reduced leave schedule may mean the employee works on a part-time arrangement. The employer must accurately keep track of how much FMLA time is used, particularly if time is taken in hourly increments or less. This will add to the administrative burden associated with FMLA.

- *Counting method.* Employers must choose the method of determining the 12-month period during which employees are eligible for 12 weeks of leave. The approach you choose must be used uniformly for all employees. Common methods used are by calendar year, fiscal year, or employee's anniversary year with the company. Although these methods are simple to understand, some companies feel they leave the company vulnerable to employees who might take 12 weeks at the end of the calendar year, then another 12 weeks right after the new year, effectively getting 24 consecutive weeks of leave. This is called leave stacking. Another approach is to start the 12-month period beginning with the first day leave is taken by the employee.

- *Paid leave.* Employers have the option of paying the employee on FMLA leave. The eligible employees may be required to draw down on accrued vacation, sick, or personal days when they receive pay during leave. Once the usual paid leave days are used up, any remaining balance of the 12-week period will be unpaid leave.

- *Medical certifications.* An employer may require that an employee's leave to care for a serious health condition be supported by a certification issued by the health care provider of the employee or the employee's ill family member.

A free copy of the FMLA can be obtained by writing to the U.S. Department of Labor, 200 Constitution Avenue N.W., Washington, DC 20210. Enclose with your request letter a label containing your return mail address. Ask for Publication 1419, *The Family and Medical Leave Act of 1993, Federal Regulations Part 825.*

Worker Adjustment and Retraining Notification Act (WARN)

Commonly known as the plant closing law, WARN specifies that employers with 100 or more full-time employees must provide advance written warning of major layoffs (60 days). The purpose of the advance notice is to help workers adjust to the impending loss of employment and start planning their job search.

Employee Polygraph Protection Act of 1988 (EPPA)

The EPPA restricts employers in the use of lie detector tests on applicants or existing employees. No employee size minimum is established.

The Occupational Safety and Health Act of 1970

This act outlines the duties of employers to protect their employees from work-related hazards. Most employers with one or more workers are covered. Employers with 11 or more employees must maintain and post logs of job-related injuries (the 200 and 101 reports) for all employees to see. Report forms can be obtained by contacting your local OSHA administration office.

Minor injuries treated by first aid are not required to be posted. You must report injuries involving death, one or more lost workdays, loss of consciousness, restricted loss of motion, injuries requiring transfer to another position, and medical treatment other than first aid.

OSHA inspectors routinely show up unannounced to inspect worksite safety conditions. The agency may be responding to a safety complaint filed by one of your own employees or investigating an accident. Unannounced visits may also be part of a scheduled inspection of preselected companies.

Inspections involve the review of OSHA 200 and 101 reports required to be maintained by the company, as well as the workplace for unsafe conditions. The inspector may require that an employee representative participate in the process with the owner.

Citations and fines may result if safety discrepancies are found. If you don't let them in, OSHA may obtain a court order to gain access.

LAWS APPLYING TO EMPLOYEE BENEFITS

The following laws are covered in this section:

Law	Company Is Covered If It Has
Consolidated Omnibus Budget Reconciliation Act (COBRA)	20 employees
The Employee Retirement Income Security Act (ERISA)	1 employee

Consolidated Omnibus Budget Reconciliation Act (COBRA)

If an employer provides health insurance coverage through the company and has 20 or more employees, it must continue to provide this coverage to terminated employees and their qualified dependents. The cost of the continued coverage is paid by the employee. Details regarding this act are addressed in Chapter 7.

The Employment Retirement Income Security Act (ERISA)

ERISA includes a whole series of rules and requirements for those employers who provide tax-qualified pension and retirement, and tax-qualified welfare plans such as health, accidental death, and disability plans. Tax qualified means that savings and interest investments in pension plans are not taxable until distributed. Under health plans, pretax income contributions toward premiums are allowed.

With regard to pensions plans, ERISA has instituted a series of complicated rules and regulations that have been designed to protect employee retirement benefits. Included are the following:

- Coverage requirements
- Eligibility and participation rules
- Vesting schedules that specify when employees are entitled to employer-paid benefits
- Limits on employer and employee contributions to pension plans
- Limits on benefits
- Pension plan funding mechanisms
- Survivor benefits
- Rules regarding termination of pension plans

The ERISA rules and regulations covering health and welfare plans (including health care, disability, and accident benefits) involve the following:

- Plan structure
- Fiduciary (financial) responsibilities
- Prohibited transactions which protect the insured
- Report and disclosure requirements

LAWS INVOLVING FEDERAL CONTRACTS OR FEDERALLY FUNDED CONTRACTS

The following laws are covered in this section:

Law	Company Is Covered If It Has
The Walsh-Healy Act	1 employee
The Davis-Bacon Act	1 employee
The Service Contract Act of 1965	1 employee
Executive Order 11246 (Affirmative Action Plans)	50 employees
The Vietnam-Era Veterans Readjustment Assistance Act of 1974	50 employees
The Rehabilitation Act of 1973	50 employees

The Walsh-Healy Act

The Walsh-Healy Act applies to federal contractors with contracts over $10,000 who provide goods and equipment to the government. Wage rates and working conditions rules may be specified.

The Davis-Bacon Act

The Davis-Bacon Act covers primarily construction contractors working on federally funded contracts doing building or repair work over $2,000. It specifies the prevailing wages that must be paid for work in particular geographic areas.

The Service Contract Act of 1965

The Service Contract Act of 1965 specifies that for service contract work over $2,500, specific prevailing wages and fringe benefits must be paid. Businesses providing services to a federal agency such as laundry, custodial, food, and guard services may be covered.

Executive Order 11246
(Affirmative Action Plans)

Executive Order 11246 covers companies with government contracts or subcontracts valued more than $10,000. This order requires written affirmative actions plans, and the company will be subject to audit by the Office of Federal Contract Compliance Programs (OFCCP).

The Vietnam-Era Veterans Readjustment
Assistance Act of 1974

The Vietnam-Era Veterans Readjustment Assistance Act of 1974 establishes requirements for businesses with federal contracts or subcontracts of $10,000 or more to list vacancies with state job services, employers with 50 or more workers and contracts of $50,000 or more must develop affirmative action plans to hire Vietnam vets.

The Rehabilitation Act of 1973

The Rehabilitation Act of 1973 specifies that businesses with federal contracts or subcontracts in excess of $2,500 must not discriminate against the handicapped. Those with 50 or more employees and a contract of more than $50,000 must have written affirmative action programs outlining their commitment to hiring minorities, women, and people with handicaps.

LABOR LAWS DEALING PRIMARILY WITH UNION RELATIONS

This section covers those laws that regulate relationships between employers, workers, and labor unions and includes the following:

Law	Company Is Is Covered If It Has
The Labor-Management Reporting and Disclosure Act (Landrum-Griffin Act)	2 employees
The Labor-Management Relations Act (Taft-Hartley Act)	2 employees

The Labor-Management Reporting and Disclosure Act (Landrum-Griffin Act)

The Labor-Management Reporting and Disclosure Act applies primarily to the regulation of unions and the protection of union members. Employers may be subject to specific reporting disclosure reporting requirements under this act, covering such areas as payments to labor consultants or loans to labor organizations.

The Labor-Management Relations Act (Taft-Hartley)

The Labor-Management Relations Act sets the ground rules for labor-related activity between employees and employers, particularly where union organizing activity is concerned. It protects the rights of employees to organize or join labor unions and addresses unfair labor practices by employers such as refusing to bargain with a union in good faith, or threats or pressure because employees engage in union organizing activities. Efforts by the employer to dominate a union may also be considered an unfair labor practice.

Union Organizing Campaigns

Union organizing campaigns are expensive, so unions normally target larger companies with more employees. Small businesses are more likely to be spared because of their size. Today, union membership represents a much smaller proportion of the U.S. workforce, about 13 to 14 percent. Nonetheless, employers should always stay alert for organizing activities, particularly if in a vulnerable industry. Many of today's union organizers are astute, highly educated people dedicated to the concept that employee interests are best represented and protected by a union.

Frequently, the early phases of an organizing campaign go unnoticed by business owners. Both inside and outside organizers operate right under their noses. When finally uncovered, management can panic, overreact to the threat, and commit an unfair labor practice, thereby jeopardizing their position.

If you encounter union activity, keep cool and consult with a labor attorney. Meanwhile, never threaten or intimidate employees because of union activity. That is illegal. Even promising them a better deal in the future can be illegal. Sending spies to their meetings is risky. There are many legal means to counter union organizing campaigns, and experts in the field are available to guide you.

STATE CIVIL LAWS
THAT CAN AFFECT EMPLOYERS

Federal civil rights laws get most of the publicity, particularly when celebrities are involved on national television. However, employees may also seek redress and damages for many employment-related grievances via the state court systems.

Breach of contract. These are lawsuits that claim an employer made written or oral agreements to abide by certain conditions of employment and later reneged, causing alleged damages to the charging employee or job applicant. To avoid trouble, refrain from comments during an employment interview that could be misconstrued as promising security in length of employment or that employees are fired only for just cause. Talk of future bonuses or pay raises can be easily or purposefully misinterpreted. Watch your tongue at open employee meetings and hiring interviews; carefully edit office memos, plant bulletins, company newsletters, employment ads, job offer letters, and employee handbooks. Have your attorney edit these documents for implied promises or other verbiage that might get you into trouble.

Negligent hiring. Customers or coworkers can hold the employer responsible if they are injured by an employee with a history of violence or crime. The employer is accused of negligence in failing to conduct background checks which would have uncovered a history of violence or illegal behavior. The theory is that if a proper investigation had been done originally, the employee would never have been hired and the injury would never have occurred.

Invasion of privacy. Invasion of privacy charges may be made concerning company drug testing programs, searches of employee belongings and vehicles, and wiretapping.

Defamation. This includes libel if the statements in question are in writing, and slander if the statements are oral. For example, an owner may be accused by a former employee of negative or false statements made in response to employment reference checks performed by a potential employer.

Intentional and/or negligent infliction of emotional distress. Owners may be charged with extreme and outrageous conduct causing severe mental and emotional distress. An example is verbal or emotional abuse.

Fraud and misrepresentation. In these cases, allegations are made that employers knowingly made false statements or promises to an employee. The employee must have relied on these statements or promises, with serious, detrimental results. A classic example would be the worker who is enticed with false information to quit his job with one company to go to another and then is unable to go back to the previous employer.

Assault and battery. These charges can arise when employees are forcibly detained on or removed from the employer's premises.

False imprisonment. Employees may claim they were unlawfully detained or restrained from leaving company premises. Such charges have been made in reaction to employer investigations of workplace theft or other unlawful activities.

Covenant of good faith and fair dealing. Some states have supported the concept that employers have an obligation to treat their employees fairly in their transactions with them, particularly when corrective action, such as firings, is taken. Employees have sued and subsequently won lawsuits claiming that they were treated unfairly. Your best protection is to ensure you administer corrective action procedures in a fair and consistent manner with everyone.

Liability in employee recreation activities. Employers may risk lawsuits involving the recreational activities they sponsor. It is wise to have adequate supervision available for these events. Ensure that proper and safe equipment is provided and that the facilities, owned or leased, are properly maintained and designed for the purpose intended. Employees should be warned of any obvious or hidden dangers of the recreational activity itself, and proper liability insurance should be carried.

Alcohol-related liability at company social functions. Liability associated with alcohol consumption has prompted many companies to stop serving alcohol altogether and some no longer sponsor annual holiday parties. Many firms reduce their liability when serving alcohol by using professional bartenders who are directed not to serve those unduly under the influence. Many companies serve food continuously but limit the time during which alcoholic beverages are served. Some supply cabs or drivers at company functions as alternative means of transportation home for people deemed intoxicated.

LEGAL POSTING REQUIREMENTS

Employers are required to post notices of many of the employment-related federal and state laws in conspicuous locations for employees and job applicants to see. If the company has more than one facility, each branch must post a set as well. Commonly placed in reception areas, break rooms, or building foyers, these notices cover minimum wage laws, OSHA, workers' compensation, child labor, unemployment, sexual harassment, civil rights, and other legislation.

Many of the required posters can be obtained from the government agencies themselves or can be purchased commercially. One company that specializes in colorful and attractive laminated posters is the g. Neil Companies, P.O. Box 450939, Sunrise, FL 33345-9982, Tel: 800-999-9111.

Guidelines for Entrepreneurs and Small Business Owners

Legal Issues

Potential for an employee lawsuit or complaint to legal authorities is always present for all employers. Quite often, it can be traced to untrained, inexperienced supervisors. Firms too small to be covered under most federal legislation may still violate some equivalent state or local employment law. The entrepreneur running the smaller business should focus on understanding and observing the following laws listed in this chapter:

- *The Fair Labor Standards Act.* Focus particularly on the overtime regulations.
- *FICA, FUTA, and SUTA laws.* Ensure that you deposit your employee social security, and unemployment taxes on time.
- *The Civil Rights Act of 1964 (Title VII).* This covers the prohibition of employment discrimination because of race, color, religion, sex, or national origin.
- *The Age Discrimination in Employment Act.*
- *The Americans with Disabilities Act.*
- *The Immigration Reform and Control Act of 1986 (IRCA).* This is particularly important if you are in an industry that traditionally employs many immigrants.

10

PERSONNEL RECORDS RETENTION AND ADMINISTRATION

The personnel files that you maintain should reflect the audit needs dictated by government legislation and the various enforcement agencies. Retention periods differ by agency, and most records are subject to on-site audits by their field representatives. Maintaining separate file categories enables cleaner, faster audits. Auditors get only need-to-know information and will appreciate not having to sort through documents not relevant to their purpose.

This chapter covers the categories, retention schedules, and governing agencies that influence how these records are filed.

PAYROLL RECORDS

The Fair Labor Standards Act (FLSA) requires that payroll records be retained for three years. These records should be kept separate from other personnel files. They are subject to on-site audit at any time by the federal Department of Labor as well as the state equivalents. Items filed in payroll records would include the following:

- Time cards and time sheets
- Forms W-4, 941, and 943 records
- Employer copies of form W-2
- Overtime records
- Commission and bonus records
- Garnishment and other wage assignment orders

THE MAIN PERSONNEL RECORDS

The main personnel records are normally filed alphabetically by employee last name. Retention time should be at least three years but it's better to keep them longer. If any legal action is pending, such as an EEOC lawsuit, these records should be retained until the action is settled. When employees leave the organization, their main personnel record can be placed in a separate section for former employees, filed alphabetically. When a former employee applies for reemployment the old record can be checked to confirm past performance and attendance history. Items usually filed in the main personnel file include the following:

- The original employment application and résumé
- A copy of the employment offer letter
- Reference check responses
- Employment test scores
- Performance reviews
- Salary history records
- Training records
- Commendation letters
- Disciplinary action memos
- Records of promotion, demotion, and transfers
- Memos of resignation
- Termination and layoff notification letters

THE I-9 RECORDS

Keep I-9 documents in alphabetical order, also filed separately. Subject to audit by the Immigration and Naturalization Service (INS), they should be retained for three years after the date the person begins work, or one year after the person's employment is terminated, whichever is later.

MEDICAL HISTORY RECORDS

It is important to keep medical history records private and separate from all other files. Maintain them alphabetically by employee. Maintained in these files are the following:

- Results of postemployment medical exams
- Copies of health benefit enrollment forms
- Workers' compensation claim records and injury reports
- Drug testing results
- Physician statements substantiating absences for sickness
- Medical documentation substantiating medical leave under the FMLA

The recommended retention time for medical records is three years, with the exception that OSHA requires medical records for employees exposed to toxic substances be kept during the employee's tenure plus 30 years.

OTHER CONSIDERATIONS

Records of Job Applicants Not Hired

Employment applications, résumés, test scores, and copies of rejection letters should be retained for a period of one year in order to comply with the Age Discrimination in Employment Act (ADEA).

File Security

Common sense dictates keeping personnel files under lock and key. Don't leave them lying around for the curious onlooker or let them out of your office. If you check them out to others on your supervisory staff, some may be lost or left unattended on a desk or workstation for others to see.

Need to Know

In most instances, the only records a supervisor will need access to in performing supervisory functions are in the main personnel file. Extra privacy precautions are needed with medical files. If medical restrictions exist that affect work performance, provide supervisors with only enough detail to assure compliance.

Personnel Records and Litigation

Once a charge has been filed, all records relevant to the charge must be maintained until final disposition has taken place. Depending on the case, relevant records may include the files of other applicants or employees with whom the charging employee is being compared.

Every document contained in employee files has the potential for becoming a legal exhibit in a court action. Owners can lose cases because of notations construed as discriminatory. Careless notes scribbled on a résumé or application referring to an applicant's race, sex, religion, and so forth are smoking guns that can cause problems if records are subpoenaed. Ensure that any documents placed in these files are clean.

Employee Access to Personnel Files

Personnel files are considered company property. Although a few states have passed laws mandating employee access, in most the decision is left up to the employer. Many firms feel permitting access is good for employee relations. If you permit access, it is recommended that the employee review his or her file in your presence. Refrain from giving the person copies, letting them make notes instead.

HUMAN RESOURCES INFORMATION SYSTEMS (HRISs)

Retrieving information from paper personnel records can be a real hassle, especially as staff size grows. In recent years, advances in computer technology have enabled the development of powerful software programs that can be run on personal computers. Prices have fallen, allowing smaller businesses with modest budgets to purchase basic HRISs. Once loaded, these systems cannot only make retrieval a snap but open up a whole new world of tools for personnel administration.

Basic HRISs

Basic or core HRISs enable a business to record and retrieve much of the personnel records information contained in the main personnel file. Once put into the system, this data can be processed and formatted into a wide variety of personnel management reports which, if created manually, would require many hours of clerical processing time.

Basic systems may contain well over one hundred standard reports which can be produced with the press of a button. Getting these reports can even become addictive because they open up new ideas for controlling and analyzing the staffing function. If the standard reports don't fulfill all your needs, many programs have the facility for creating custom-designed reports as well.

Basic HRISs contain fields that facilitate storing, tracking, and reporting the following types of information:

- Employee personal information such as name, address, and telephone numbers
- Current job and salary information; prior pay and job history
- Performance review data
- Basic benefits information, including benefit options selected by the employee
- Dependent information and emergency contact name and addresses

- Records of employee skills
- OSHA and workers' compensation accident data

Once loaded with pertinent data, basic programs can compile individual employee data into standard reports for the company as a whole, or broken down further by unit, cost, or profit center levels. Some of the standard reports include the following:

- *Employee information reports* such as age lists, birthday lists, home mailing labels, employee counts, skills and education, work telephone directory, and organization list by company or unit
- *Compensation and performance reports* such as ranked salary lists; salary history; analysis by job code, title, or grade; performance review due dates; new-hire and termination logs; turnover statistics; and employee longevity reports
- *Benefits administration reports* including coverage and enrollment data for benefits and 401(k) plans, census data reports for insurance, COBRA billing statements and notification letters, employee dependent lists, and workers' compensation and OSHA injury reports

More powerful options can be included in basic systems to track attendance, providing absence averages for units, for the company, and for individual employees.

Add-On Features

As a business grows in size and sophistication, add-on modules can be purchased from the same HRIS vendor to supplement the core system. These modules are integrated with one another in that they share common data elements contained in the basic system, excluding the need for duplicate data entry.

Payroll Processing

A payroll processing module can be added when it is decided to do payroll internally. An important advantage of payroll modules is that they integrate personnel and payroll systems into one, eliminating the need for duplicate records and data entry. It is estimated that approximately one-third of employee information contained in the personnel files is also needed to run payroll.

Payroll modules facilitate quick time sheet entry, sharing of benefits information for payroll deductions, and automatic withholding adjustments as benefits and premiums change according to salary, seniority, age, or dependent status. They do automatic accrual of leave, tax withholding processing, and a whole series of payroll, time, and labor reports including 941, 1099, and W-2 reports.

Benefits Administration

These modules contain programs written to track benefit plans such as health, life, 401(k) and other defined contribution retirement plans, flexible spending accounts, and so forth. They expand on the benefit features within the core program and contain built-in enrollment forms and confirmation notices. They will automatically communicate benefit change information to the payroll module.

Position Control Systems (PCSs)

PCSs assist management in personnel planning and budgeting. They track positions and costs, and provide actual versus authorized job counts, projected labor costs by unit, division, or company. They also provide vacancy and turnover rates, open positions, budgeted versus actual salary changes, position vacancy time, and other elements.

Training Administration Modules

Training administration modules assist in enrolling trainees in classes, produce class rosters and schedules, maintain training catalogs, and keep track of certifications required by employees. They have reporting features for both custom and standard reports and can generate reports on class attendance, class histories, and other training-related activities.

Guidelines for Entrepreneurs and Small Business Owners

Personnel Records Retention and Administration

- Privacy is essential when it comes to personnel files, particularly with medical records information.
- Keep personnel records under lock and key with access only on a strict need-to-know basis.
- Remember, everything within an employee's personnel file can be disclosed to outside parties in the course of employee lawsuits.
- Computer software for personnel files is getting cheaper. Consider adding an HRIS linked with your payroll system if you grow larger—say, 50 or more employees.

11

RECRUITING A HUMAN RESOURCES ADMINISTRATOR

Historically, the position of human resources (HR) administrator evolves over time as entrepreneurs delegate personnel tasks to an administrative assistant, the payroll clerk, or perhaps the controller. Some firms create an office manager position, combining personnel administration with facilities services, purchasing, a travel desk, and other related administrative support functions.

This combined approach may work for a while, but with further growth the people issues become more prevalent. Staying current with the changing regulations involving employment, benefits, compensation and the EEOC becomes more difficult. The office manager starts to bog down, or the controller, inundated with tax audits or year-end closings, can't keep up.

Over time, the need for a full-time HR administrator becomes more obvious to the owner. Fortunately, most firms reach this conclusion as part of normal growth and expansion. Others are shocked into it, realizing that an expensive lawsuit may possibly have been avoided had effective personnel management controls been in place.

The requirement for a full-time HR person is closely linked to the number of employees within the company. Historically, the ratio of one HR person for every 100 employees was the standard, with variations depending on the industry, organization structure, and geographic dispersion.

With advances in telecommunications and the trend toward downsizing, fewer HR people are expected to support more employees. As a result, the pressure is on for HR professionals to become proficient in more than one personnel specialty.

HR practitioners are also required to become versed in disciplines such as production, finance, and marketing. The more progressive entrepreneurs recognize that employees are vital to corporate success, and expect human resources to play a more active role in managing personnel assets in partnership with line management. HR *must* have a good grasp of operational matters in order to win management support. This new emphasis is reflected in company organization charts, with HR often reporting directly to the owner/CEO.

When you decide to hire an HR administrator you'll have many available candidates from which to choose. The field is so broad that few will be expert in all facets. People enter the field from a variety of gateways. Applicants may range from administrative assistants who work their way up the ranks to university graduates with advanced degrees in labor relations. There is no magic formula to use in making the right choice for your company. You can narrow your search, however, by considering each applicant's experience, skills, and education.

EXPERIENCE

Smaller businesses running ads for their first HR generalist will often seek two to three years of experience; consider seeking five. Becoming competent in the main HR functions takes more than 2 or 3 years. Additional time is needed to get good hands-on exposure to working through the many problems and issues involved in recruiting, benefits administration, compensation, employee relations, and training.

CRITICAL SKILLS

A higher standard of personal integrity, patience, and sensitivity are essential ingredients in order for an HR administrator to operate effectively. Both owners and employees must feel secure that human resources will maintain confidentiality when appropriate. Most employees hold HR people to higher standards of personal behavior. As interviewers, counselors, policy writers, and trainers, excellent oral and written communications skills are essential. Reasonable proficiency in numerical skills (business math, algebra, and some statistics) is needed for working with compensation programs. Proficiency with personal computers is important, particularly with regard to word processing functions, spreadsheets, and the ability to organize, input to and extract information from a computer database. Someone who is comfortable with HRISs would be ideal.

EDUCATION

Requiring a college degree may improve your chances of attracting candidates with some of the skills listed above and cut down on the résumé pile. The downside is that it may also eliminate well-qualified candidates with considerable practical HR experience learned through on-the-job training. When screening résumés, look for a variety of professional certifications common to the HR field.

Note: If you are in the process of developing one of your existing employees for a human resources position, certification programs are a good place to start.

Professional in Human Resources (PHR) and Senior Professional in Human Resources (SPHR)

The PHR and SPHR designations are awarded to HR practitioners who have passed a written comprehensive examination and have verified years of exempt-level experience within the field. Four years of experience is required for the PHR without a bachelor's degree, two years with one, and one year with a graduate degree. Eight years of experience is required for the SPHR without a bachelor's, six years with one, and five years with a graduate degree.

The program is sponsored by the Society for Human Resources Management (SHRM).

Certified Employee Benefits Specialist (CEBS)

The CEBS program is cosponsored by the Wharton School and International Foundation of Employee Benefit Plans. In order to obtain certification you must pass ten college-level courses covering a broad spectrum of employee benefits administration, including health and welfare plans, pension plans, stock plans, and so forth. Courses can be taken at cooperating universities nationwide.

Certified Compensation Professional (CCP)

The CCP program is sponsored by the American Compensation Association (ACA). The latest requirement for anyone just entering the program is to pass nine examinations covering a variety of compensation subjects. The core program consists of participation in seminars that last two and one-half days with an exam taken on the third day. Two courses have recently been formatted for self-study at home via computer or workbook material.

Certified Benefits Professional (CBP)

The CBP program is also sponsored by the American Compensation Association. It requires passing nine exams covering benefit-related subjects and parallels the procedures of the CCP program.

Certification Program Information

For more information about the certification programs described here, contact the following organizations:

PHR/SPHR Programs:	**CCP/CBP Programs:**
Human Resource Certification Institute	American Compensation Association
606 N. Washington Street	P.O. Box 29312

Alexandria, VA 22314
Telephone: 703-548-3440
Fax: 703-836-0367

Phoenix, AZ 85038-9312
Tel: 602-922-2020
Fax: 602-483-8352

CEBS Program:
18700 W. Blue Mound Rd., P.O. Box 1270
Brookfield, WI 53008-1270
Telephone: 414-786-6700
Fax: 414-786-6647

CANDIDATE SOURCES

Often, local chapters of the Society for Human Resources Management (SHRM), the American Compensation Association (ACA), and Certified Employee Benefits Specialists (CEBS) will operate résumé referral services on behalf of their members seeking work. If you give them a call, they'll send you résumés (in confidence) of members seeking employment. To help you with your search, Figure 11-1 provides a sample HR ad, and Figure 11-2 provides a job description for an HR administrator.

Figure 11-1   Human Resources Administrator Ad

Human Resources Administrator

Growing company located in NE Atlanta
seeks HR Administrator with a minimum 5 years'
experience in Personnel Administration, including compensation and
benefits, employment, employee relations, and
training. Requires good knowledge of federal and
state employment law. HR certifications a
plus. Mail or fax résumé to
Ad #166___
Journal-Constitution
P.O. Box 4666
Atlanta, GA 30066
Fax: 404-555-1212

Figure 11-2   Job Description for Human Resources Administrator

Job Description

Title: Human Resources Administrator   **FLSA Status:** Exempt

General Summary:
Responsible for the daily administration of personnel policies and procedures for the company. Major functions are employment, compensation and benefits administration, employee relations, employee services, legal compliance, and personnel records administration.

Essential Duties and Responsibilities:
1. Administers wage and salary and performance appraisal programs for the company.
2. Administers employee benefits, including health, life, disability, worker's compensation insurance programs. Maintains company vacation and leave programs.
3. Monitors company legal compliance programs pertaining to EEO, IRCA, ADA, FMLA; stays current with changes in employment-related laws and rulings.
4. Administers employee relations activities, including the investigation and review of employee grievances; compliance with disciplinary action procedures; company-sponsored awards and employee social activities programs.
5. Responsible for recruitment activities such as running ads, applicant screening and interviewing, administration of employment tests, reference checks, generation of employment and rejection letters.
6. Maintains personnel records and retention systems.

Nonessential Duties and Responsibilities:
1. Assists telephone switchboard operator/receptionist as needed.
2. Assists in interoffice mail distribution as required.
3. Orders stock, replenishes stock supplies weekly.

Job Specifications:
1. Excellent knowledge of employment laws and regulations.
2. General knowledge of traditional compensation and employee benefit programs.
3. Excellent verbal and written communication skills.
4. Competent PC skills (word processing/spreadsheet).
5. Excellent interpersonal skills.
6. Ability to maintain confidentiality.
7. Effective conflict resolution skills.

Working Conditions:
Work is primarily performed in a private office environment with frequent telephone interruptions. Daily visits to the manufacturing floor are required where sound protection is needed because of high decibel noise levels. Travel via airline required once a month to west coast facility.

The above information has been designed to indicate the general nature and level of work performed by employees within this classification. It is not designed to contain or be interpreted as a comprehensive inventory of all duties, responsibilities, and qualifications required of employees assigned to this job.

Guidelines for Entrepreneurs
and Small Business Owners

Recruiting a Human Resources Administrator

In a small firm, the owner, office administrator, or payroll person normally handles day-to-day human resources functions. If you grow large enough, say, anywhere from 85 to 100 employees, you're probably ready for a full-time human resources administrator. Whether you promote someone from within the company or recruit a person from the outside, keep the following in mind.

No matter how experienced and effective the HR person may be, that person's contribution to your operations will be limited by how much support you, the entrepreneur, ultimately give them. This is because HR is a staff function and can easily get sidetracked by more immediate and pressing business demands.

Don't hesitate to require that the HR administrator become familiar with your other business operations. An HR administrator who gets to know your business will be able to do the HR job much better. His or her credibility in your eyes and those of your other employees will be that much higher.

GLOSSARY

accidental death and dismemberment insurance (AD&D): Insurance coverage for loss of life, limbs, or eyesight resulting from an accident.

Age Discrimination and Employment Act (ADEA): A federal antidiscrimination law to protect job applicants and employees age 40 and over from employment discrimination because of their age. Includes discrimination involving pay, benefits, and other conditions of employment.

alternative dispute resolution (ADR): Resolving employee grievances via means other than judicial systems, for example, through arbitration or mediation.

American Compensation Association (ACA): A not-for-profit association of professionals engaged in the design, implementation, and management of employee compensation and benefit programs.

Americans with Disabilities Act (ADA): A federal antidiscrimination law designed to remove barriers that prevent qualified individuals with disabilities from enjoying the same employment opportunities that are available to persons without disabilities.

broad banding: The technique of consolidating salary grades into wider or broader bands to create more flexible pay structures.

Bureau of Labor Statistics (BLS): A bureau within the federal Department of Labor responsible for collecting national labor statistics for wage and salary surveys.

cafeteria plans: All employees are provided basic core benefits such as health, life, disability, and retirement benefits but are also allocated additional dollars with which they can purchase additional benefits to supplement core benefits.

Certified Benefits Professional (CBP): Compensation and benefits professionals who have successfully completed the benefits certification program of the American Compensation Association.

Certified Compensation Professional (CCP): Compensation and benefits professionals who have successfully completed the compensation certification program of the American Compensation Association (ACA).

Certified Employee Benefits Specialists (CEBS): Benefits professionals who have successfully completed the benefits certification program sponsored by the Wharton School and International Benefits Society.

Civil Rights Act of 1964—Title VII: The major federal civil rights law prohibiting discrimination in employment because of race, color, religion, sex, or national origin.

Civil Rights Act of 1991 (CRA): A federal civil rights law that provides for compensatory and punitive damages in cases of intentional discrimination, and jury trials.

coinsurance: Insurance benefits plans that require the insured to pay some part of covered claim expenses, for example, 20 percent out-of-pocket payment by the insured, 80 percent payment by the insurer.

compensable factors: A term used in job evaluation denoting criteria for comparing worth between jobs. Examples are skill, effort, responsibility, and working conditions.

Consolidated Omnibus Budget Reconciliation Act of 1985 (COBRA): A federal law regulating benefits. One of its major components requires continuation of an employer's group health benefits for terminated employees and their eligible dependents under specified circumstances.

cost of living adjustment (COLA): Salary increases for all or for a class of employees because of inflation.

Davis-Bacon Act: A federal law applying to employers with government contracts and that requires prevailing wages.

deductibles: Out-of-pocket dollars insureds are responsible for before insurance benefits are payable. Primarily used in health insurance plans.

employee assistance plan (EAP): A program sponsored by the employer to assist in the identification and resolution of productivity problems associated with employees impaired by personal problems with marital, family, financial, alcohol, drug, legal, emotional, or other personal matters.

Employee Retirement Income Security Act of 1974 (ERISA): A federal law that regulates private employer pension and welfare plans.

Equal Employment Opportunity Commission (EEOC): Created by Congress, it enforces Title VII of the Civil Rights Act of 1964, the Age Discrimination in Employment Act, the Equal Pay Act, Section 501 of the Rehabilitation Act, and the Americans with Disabilities Act.

Equal Pay Act of 1963: An amendment to the Fair Labor Standards Act of 1938, it prohibits sex-based wage discrimination between men and women in the same establishment who are performing under similar working conditions.

Executive Order 11246: Requires firms with federal contracts or subcontracts to implement written affirmative action plans to increase minority and female participation in the workplace.

exempt employees: Those employees who are working in positions that are considered exempt from the minimum wage and overtime requirements of the Fair Labor Standards Act (FLSA). Examples include managers, supervisors, and outside salespeople.

Fair Employment Practice Agencies (FEPAs): Under Title VII and the ADA, the EEOC must defer charges of discrimination to state or local Fair Employment Practice Agencies. The charge may be processed initially by either the EEOC or a state or local agency, if a work-sharing agreement so specifies.

Fair Labor Standards Act of 1938 (FLSA): A federal law mandating the minimum wage, overtime pay, equal pay for men and women in the same type of job, child labor regulations, and record-keeping requirements.

The Family and Medical Leave Act of 1993 (FMLA): A federal law that requires private sector employers of 50 or more employees, and public agencies to provide up to 12 workweeks of unpaid leave to eligible employees for certain specified family and medical reasons; to maintain preexisting group health insurance during periods of FMLA leave; and to restore eligible employees to their same or an equivalent position at the conclusion of their FMLA leave.

Federal Insurance Contributions Act (FICA): Legislation that established requirements for payroll withholding and matching employer contributions to the social security program.

fee for service: A traditional means of compensating physicians for medical/surgical services performed. Fees vary according to specific procedures performed, or the usual, customary, and reasonable fees scheduled by an insurance carrier.

flexible spending accounts (FSAs): An arrangement in which employees are permitted under IRS regulations to contribute specific percentages of pretax wages to an individual spending account for reimbursement of eligible health or child care expenses.

flextime: A flexible working arrangement whereby employees are present during core working hours but have the flexibility of arriving and departing at different times each day, provided the required hours are worked each week.

garnishment: A court order directing an employer to deduct a specific amount from an employee's wages to pay for debts owed to an outside creditor. The employer is responsible for remitting the money to the creditor or court.

green circle rate: A salary rate that is below the minimum of its salary range.

human resources information systems (HRISs): Computerized personnel management and records systems covering all major HR operations including compensation and benefits, manpower planning, payroll administration, training, government reporting, and so on.

I-9 form: The employment eligibility form which must be completed by new employees and employers in order to conform to INS regulations.

Immigration and Naturalization Service (INS): The agency within the U.S. Department of Justice responsible for controlling legal and illegal immigration of foreigners within the country. The INS will audit employers to assure compliance with INS regulations regarding employment of alien nationals in the United States.

Immigration Reform and Control Act of 1986: Controls illegal immigration to the United States and prohibits employment of unauthorized foreign nationals.

interquartile range: In an ordered series of numbers, the distance between the third quartile and the first quartile. It contains the middle 50 percent of data.

Labor-Management Relations Act of 1947 (Taft-Hartley Act): Defines labor relations rights of both employees and employers, prohibits unfair labor practices, and specifies collective bargaining rights.

managed care: A health care delivery system stressing preventive health care in a group practice environment. Includes HMO, PPO, and IPA systems.

management by objectives: A technique in which management and employees work together in setting goals for the forthcoming performance review period.

median: The middle number in a set of numbers arrayed from highest to lowest.

multirater assessments: A performance rating technique that includes evaluations from other persons in addition to an employee's immediate superior. Input may be obtained from peers, subordinates, teamworkers, even customers to form the overall evaluation.

nonexempt employees: Employees in positions that require compliance with the overtime and minimum wage requirements of the Fair Labor Standards Act (FLSA).

The Occupational Safety and Health Act of 1970: Federal legislation setting forth the occupational safety and health hazard standards and requirements for employers.

Old Age, Survivors, Disability, and Health Insurance Program (OASDHI): Federal legislation primarily enabling the operation of the social security and medicare programs.

percentile: Numerical values that define the value below which a given percentage of the data fall (i.e., the 75th percentile is the point below which 75 percent of the data falls). Used in evaluating wage surveys and salary ranges.

point factor evaluation: A job evaluation system using numerical point values to compare and evaluate the worth of different positions.

point of service plans (POS): Health insurance plans enabling the insured to have the option of choosing managed care services or out-of-network care. Out-of-network services normally require coinsurance amounts since they are usually more expensive.

position control systems (PCSs): Automated computer-based systems that enable management to plan, budget, and control staffing.

premium sharing: Employees share a percentage of the cost of group monthly premium costs with their employer.

Professional in Human Resources (PHR): Certification awarded to HR professionals who pass an exam and meet the experience and education requirements specified by the Society for Human Resource Management (SHRM).

red circle rate: A salary rate above the maximum for its salary range.

Rehabilitation Act of 1973: Federal legislation prohibiting employers with federal contracts from discriminating against the handicapped. Requires employers to have written affirmative action plans for hiring the handicapped.

salary midpoint: The rate halfway between the minimum and maximum of the salary range.

Senior Human Resources Professional (SPHR): Certification awarded to HR professionals who pass an exam and meet the experience and educational requirements specified by the Society for Human Resources Management (SHRM).

Vietnam-Era Veterans Readjustment Act: Federal legislation requiring employers with federal contracts or subcontracts to take affirmative action in hiring Vietnam-era vets.

weighted average: Calculated by weighting each individual average by the number of salaries in the set. Also known as the weighted mean.

Worker Adjustment and Retraining Notification Act (WARN): Federal law requiring employers with 100 or more employees to provide advance warning of plant closings.

INDEX

Entrepreneur *Magazine* **FREE ADVICE**

WHEN WAS THE LAST TIME YOU GOT FREE ADVICE THAT WAS WORTH ANYTHING?

Entrepreneur Magazine, the leading small business authority, is loaded with free advice—small business advice that could be worth millions to you. Every issue gives you detailed, practical knowledge on how to start a business and run it successfully. *Entrepreneur* is the perfect resource to keep small business owners up to date and on track. Whether you're looking for a new business or already own one, *Entrepreneur* will advise you how to build it better.

To get your share of free advice from *Entrepreneur* and receive your **FREE ISSUE**, Call 800-864-6868, Dept. 54CE3, or mail this coupon to: Entrepreneur Magazine, 2392 Morse Avenue, Irvine, CA 92714

Get your FREE ISSUE of Entrepreneur today!

12 issues of ENTREPRENEUR for just $9.99

☐**YES!** Start my subscription to *Entrepreneur Magazine*.
I get a full year's worth for **just $9.99**—that's 50% off the regular subscription price and almost 74% off the newsstand rate.

Name:_____
(please print)
Address: _____
City: _____
State/Zip:_____

Entrepreneur.

Please allow 4-6 weeks for delivery of first issue.
Offer good in U.S. only. Canadian and foreign prices on request.

RUNAWAY SUCCESS!
Make your business a powerful success. Keep it running with ENTREPRENEUR.

For faster service, call 800-274-6229, Dept. 54CF1

54CF1

Entrepreneur
THE SMALL BUSINESS AUTHORITY

ORDER YOUR NOW! FREE ISSUE

And Get FREE Advice To Help Run Your Business

☐**YES!** Send me my FREE issue of *Entrepreneur.*

Name _____
(please print)

Address: _____

City: _____

State/Zip: _____

54CE3

Mail coupon to: Entrepreneur Magazine, Dept. 54CE3, 2392 Morse Avenue, Irvine, CA 92714

96
Banks
Eager To
Give You
Money

FREE!

Make Your Business a Runaway Success.
Keep it running with Entrepreneur

50% OFF

In the pages of *Entrepreneur,* you find the information you need to keep your business running smoothly—everything from financial advice and marketing tips to management techniques and government regulations. *Entrepreneur* is an ongoing, up-to-date resource for small business owners who want to stay abreast of the issues without spending hours and hours seeking out important information.

Don't miss this opportunity to save 50% off the regular subscription price. To order your half-price subscription today,

call 800-274-6229, Dept. 54CF1

Entrepreneur® *or send this coupon to:*
P. O. Box 50368, Boulder,CO 80321-0368.

ENTREPRENEUR MAGAZINE PRESENTS

AEA.

AMERICAN ENTREPRENEURS ASSOCIATION

Get big business advantages from the #1 small business network.

Succeeding in business doesn't come easy. It takes resources...connections... inside information...things only larger companies used to have access to.UNTIL NOW!

The American Entrepreneurs Association, established by Entrepreneur Magazine Group, is a nationwide network organization dedi-cated to providing small business with big business advantages.

- Receive numerous AEA members-only benefits and discounts.
- Network with other small business owners.
- Over 30,000 members.
- Communicate with experts that can help you grow your business.

Call Toll-Free: (800) 421-2300, Dept. MJWK Join Today—Just $12.00!

Create a BETTER Business Plan with your computer

Entrepreneur Magazine's

Developing a Successful Business Plan Software

Designed by a team of senior business executives and the editors of *Entrepreneur Magazine*, this easy-to-use software program takes you step-by-step through the creation of a comprehensive business plan. • Organize your thoughts before you spend time and money on a new business idea.

JUST $49.50! ORDER TODAY.

• Prepare your plan for presentation to others and anticipate their questions and objections. • Impress bankers, prospective partners, landlords and vendors with a complete, professionally-prepared business plan.

ACT NOW! Be A Member For Just $12.00

AEA Members-Only Roster of Benefits

- 25-40% discount on long distance calls
- Freight discounts with Airborne Express
- Toll-free deep-discount travel hotline
- Affordable health care
- Lowest published air fares via computerized reservation system
- Toll-free travel counseling and reservations service
- Discounts on hotels, rental cars, cruises

- Bimonthly AEA Exchange newsletter
- 50% discount on Entrepreneur Magazine
- $10 discount on all Business Guides
- Discounts on all other 150 products in Entrepreneur's Small Business Catalog
- FREE admission to Entrepreneur's Small Business Expos and Workshops
- 20% discount on CompuServe membership kit
- Wallet card with convenient phone numbers

Get these benefits and more when you join the AEA. Call today!

(800) 421-2300, Dept. MJWK

Or mail your check for only $12.00 payable to:
American Entrepreneurs Association, Dept. MJWK 2392 Morse Avenue, Irvine, CA 92714

Entrepreneur Magazine

ORDER YOUR BUSINESS PLAN SOFTWARE NOW!

Entrepreneur

Just call toll-free (800) 421-2300, Dept. MJWB or send this coupon along with your check to:
ENTREPRENEUR MAGAZINE,
P. O. Box 1625, Des Plaines, IL 60017-1625.

Name:_____

Address:_____

City:_____

State/Zip: _____

Add $6.75 for shipping & handling. CA residents add 7.75% sales tax.

JUST $49.50!
ORDER TODAY.

Developing a Successful Business Plan Software

SELECT SOFTWARE FORMAT BY CODE:	
8049 (PC) 5.25"	8050 (Windows) 5.25"
8349 (PC) 3.5"	8350 (Windows) 3.5"
8549 (Macintosh)	

MJWB